CRUSADERS
-OF-
MIGHT AND MAGIC™
Prima's Official Strategy Guide

3DO™

Prima Publishing© and the Prima logo are registered trademarks of Prima Communications, Inc.

Prima Games, A Division of Prima Communications, Inc.
3000 Lava Ridge Ct.
Roseville, CA 95661
(916)787-7000
www.primagames.com

ISBN: 0-7615-2432-0
Library of Congress Catalog Card Number: 9965389
Printed in the United States of America

00 01 02 03 GG 10 9 8 7 6 5 4 3 2 1

and Incan Monkey God Studios are trademarks of IMGS, Inc.
www.incanmonkey.com

TABLE OF CONTENTS

CREDITS

Editor	David Ladyman, Melissa Tyler
Writers	Chris McCubbin, Tuesday Frase, David Ladyman, Beth Loubet, Anthony Salter
Template Design	Winter Graphics North
Design & Layout	Raini Madden, Jennifer Spohrer
Prima Product Mgr.	Renée Middleton
Prima Project Edtr.	Brooke Raymond
Game Artists	Yu-fen Croddy, Paul Forest, Marc Apablaza, Klee Miller, Chip Patterson, Jeff Perryman, Chris Sellers, Michael Wallin, David Wells, Michael Kennedy, Sara Szundi
Special Thanks	David Georgeson, David Downing, Eric Brown, Bruce Adams, Scott McDaniel

DRAKE

DRAKE

CRUSADER FIELD DISPATCH, FOR THE COMMANDER'S EYES ONLY

Lady Celestia,

I have made much progress in the task you set me to, yet there is much about this Drake which remains obscure. It seems that every fact I learn about the young man raises two or three new and unexpected questions. Sadly, I feel that much remains to be discovered before I can at last seize that one central fact which will make all of the contradictory elements of my subject's character fall into place.

I have heard numerous accounts of Drake's origins. In fact, for one so young, the number of wild legends that have already sprung up around his name is nothing short of astounding. Most of these can be disregarded out of hand, either because they are overtly superstitious nonsense (several stories which make Drake the son/nephew/brother of Necros) or because they contravene known facts (any stories which have Drake already acting on behalf of the Order). There are two persistent rumors that I consider more likely. The first says that Drake was a child during the early incursions of the Legion, and that his family was slain in battle, moving Drake to a life of revenge. The second rumor has it that Drake is the disgraced son of a nobleman (the identity of this hypothetical parent varies with the teller) who has taken up a life of errantry in order to prove his worth to his family.

Health	100
Mana	100
Strength	30
Speed	Average
Melee Bonus	0
Ranged Bonus	0

I have been able to confirm that Drake lived for several years with Nomandi the Stoic, the scholar and honored hero of our Order. I have traveled to the monastery that Nomandi used for a hermitage, and there I found written records, in the sage's own hand, that Drake stayed their several years as Nomandi's student and companion. I also found a gravestone in the old sanctuary, crudely but carefully inscribed with Nomandi's name, and dated just over three years ago. I confess that I did not confirm the contents of the grave myself, having no desire to disturb the rest of the old hero. I am sure you have already discerned that the time recorded for Nomandi's death closely matches the beginning of Drake's most recent and most impressive adventures.

Regarding those adventures, I must confess myself surprised to find that the evidence that I have so far uncovered tends to confirm that Drake actually performed most of the improbable deeds attributed to him. Specifically, he was present at, and quite likely responsible for, the burning of the Legion camp at Highmeadow, the inexplicably aborted siege of Dormir, and the Crusaders' retreat from the Erngard observation post, which was made possible by an unexpected delay in the advancing Legion forces. I've also linked him to numerous reports of disrupted Legion patrols and villagers or freeholders saved or warned of Legion assaults.

Finally, I am pleased to report that I have made personal contact with the subject.

I was pursuing my inquiries in the town of Cador Sul. I had already been two nights at their inn when the innkeeper greeted me upon my arrival one evening with, "You were asking about Drake? Well, he's sitting over there."

Turning to the indicated table, I observed a young man, apparently of somewhat less than 30 years. I could not guess his age more precisely, for his skin was darkened and weathered by outdoor living. He was not overly large, but powerfully muscled. His hair and eyes were both dark, and his countenance was well favored, except for a jagged scar that cut across his cheek. His clothes were sturdy and plain, well suited for travelling and fighting (in fact, he was dressed after the fashion of travelling operatives of our Order, and in this I perceived the hand of Nomandi). He was carrying a longsword, which I never saw unsheathed, but the scabbard and hilt were both solidly made, apparently well maintained, and devoid of ornamentation.

I took a pint to a nearby table, and for much of the evening I merely sat and listened to him conversing with the locals. He seemed perfectly at ease among the townsfolk, and his accent was that of a common farmer (if he is indeed a noble's son, he hides it well). By his conversation I discerned a certain native intelligence, but little refinement or culture. His wit, however, was ready and surprisingly caustic. (He offered up one involved and very effective anecdote concerning yourself, Lady Celestia, which I had not heard before, and which I look forward to sharing when next we meet, as I know you collect such things.) He displayed little love for authority of any kind, and was particularly dismissive of our Order. However, he also spoke quite satirically of the Legion. I received the distinct impression that the townsfolk came away from their conversation much heartened by his presence.

In short, he seemed much like many a young bravo of the sort you might find at the mess tables of the High Guard, with one exception. Young warriors, as you well know, Lady, are much given to boasting of their prowess. Indeed, it is for many their greatest love and primary recreation. Drake, however, steadfastly refused to speak of himself at all, either his prior adventures, or his future plans, or his present business. All such inquiries were waved away with a smile and a quip.

I remained in the common room until Drake went up to his lodging. I was resolved to present myself to him the next morning, away from the crowd of admiring townspeople. However, though I rose the next morning before the first scullery maid was up, I waited in vain for Drake to arise. I later discovered that he had slept only a few short hours, and departed that place in the middle of the night, which I was told by the innkeeper was his usual practice when visiting civilization.

XPERIENCE

at is experience?
tty much what you'd guess — credit for
ing things and completing quests.

w much experience do I get for killing
ething?

h foe has an experience value, listed in its
ividual stats and in the stat table on pp.
3-111. Each foe also has a "level" assigned
t. If you're at the same level as what you
you get credit for exactly that much expe-
ice. For example, if you kill a Dasher
iger (level 5) while you're at experience
el 5, you get exactly 2500 experience.

wever, if you kill a higher-level foe, you
credit for even more experience. If you're
evel 2 when you kill the Ranger, you get a
% bonus — 3500 experience, rather than
t 2500. On the other hand, if you kill a
that's three levels lower than you, you
y get credit for 60% of the listed value —
)0, rather than 2500.

at does experience give me?

you gain experience (XP), you gain experience levels. With each new level, your
ilth, Mana and Strength increase. More often than not, you also get a higher damage
us (when you strike in melee or ranged combat).

Foe's Level – Drake's Level	Experience Multiplier
6 or more	3.0
5	2.0
4	1.8
3	1.4
2	1.2
1	1.1
0	1.0
-1	0.9
-2	0.8
-3	0.6
-4	0.3
-5	0.1
-6 or less	No experience

Positive numbers mean the foe is tougher than Drake. Negative numbers mean the foe is weaker than Drake.

Here's the chart of what happens as you gain each new level:

Drake's Level	Drake's XP Total	Max Health	Max Mana	Strength	Melee Damage Bonus	Ranged Damage Bonus
Start	0	100	100	30	–	–
1	8,000	121	116	32	–	–
2	16,800	146	135	34	–	–
3	27,280	177	156	36	+10%	–
4	40,488	214	181	38	+20%	–
5	57,745	259	210	40	+20%	+5%
6	80,776	314	244	42	+30%	+5%
7	111,885	380	283	44	+30%	+5%
8	154,182	459	328	46	+40%	+5%
9	211,898	556	380	48	+50%	+5%
10	290,803	673	441	50	+50%	+10%
11	398,789	814	512	52	+50%	+10%
12	546,654	985	594	54	+70%	+10%
13	749,184	1192	689	56	+70%	+10%
14	1,026,632	1442	799	58	+70%	+10%
15	1,406,744	1745	927	60	+80%	+15%

HINT

Character Development

Crusaders of Might and Magic requires a long view for success. You have to think not just about whether you'll be able to survive the monsters around the next corner, but also whether you'll still be able to survive the much tougher monsters three or four quests down the road.

You advance in three ways throughout the game. First, you advance by increasing your overall experience level. You gain experience by defeating foes.

Second, by finding significant items like talismans, armor, weapons, shields and spells. More and more powerful weapons and armor make you tougher overall.

Finally, you must individually increase your skill with weapons and spells. There are up to 15 ranks of proficiency with each weapon (see pp. 12-13), and up to five ranks for each spell (see pp. 17-20).

Your magic and combat skills are increased through actually using them in combat. *There are not enough fights in the game to allow you to get to maximum level in everything.* However, to survive and triumph at the end of the game, you'll need to "max out" your most important skills. Recognizing what those skills are, and managing their development sensibly, is a major part of the long-term strategy of the game.

The limited amount of experience in the game is yet another reason to engage and destroy any foe you happen across (see *Be Aggressive*, p. 9) rather than outrunning or evading it, as long as you have a reasonable chance of survival. Don't get impatient and start blowing past those "easy" creatures you know you can take, either. Such low-key fights offer you an important opportunity to either optimize you key skills, or to get a little extra "oomph" in secondary skills that are useful at medium level. And anytime you fight, you gain overall experience.

DRAKE

Weapon Ranks

What is a weapon rank?

Whenever you strike with a weapon *and* it causes even one point of damage to a foe, then you gain "weapon experience" with that weapon. You accumulate experience in each individual weapon, so you get better with the weapon(s) that you use most often — more experience means a higher "weapon rank."

Each weapon strike that inflicts damage adds 10 points of weapon experience to that weapon's ranking. However, this swing is modified according to the Experience Multiplier chart on 4, so that you get less experience against feeble opponents, and you learn more from stronger opponents.

What does a higher weapon rank do for me?

Weapon skill ranks increase the weapon's damage and (for melee weapons) how fast you can strike with that weapon. These multipliers are *in addition* to your regular experience level bonus. If you're at experience level 3 and have weapon rank 5 with your mace, you get a 40% damage bonus (10% + 30%) with every blow.

Weapon Rank	Weapon Experience Required	Melee Damage Bonus	Melee Speed Bonus	Ranged Damage Bonus
Start	0	–	–	–
1	500	+10%	–	–
2	1,050	+10%	+10%	–
3	1,705	+20%	+10%	–
4	2,531	+20%	+20%	–
5	3,609	+30%	+20%	+5%
6	5,049	+30%	+30%	+5%
7	6,993	+40%	+30%	+5%
8	9,636	+40%	+40%	+5%
9	13,244	+50%	+40%	+5%
10	18,175	+50%	+50%	+10%
11	24,924	+10%	+50%	+10%
12	34,166	+60%	+60%	+10%
13	46,824	+70%	+60%	+10%
14	64,165	+70%	+70%	+10%
15	87,921	+80%	+70%	+15%

HINT

Weapon Skills

The most important thing about developing your armed combat is to have a weapon skill "maxed out" by the end of the game. Since it's not possible to max out every weapon, it's important that you pick one early on and concentrate your efforts on developing it.

Which weapon is best? Playtesters were divided between the longsword and the battle axe. The sword offers good speed and damage throughout the entire game. The axe offers maximum damage at the end of the game, but its low speed can be a major handicap early on.

pell Ranks

at is a spell rank?

enever you successfully cast a spell (interrupted casts do not count), *regardless* of
ther it does damage, then you gain experience with that spell. You gain experience in
 individual spell, so you get better with the spells that you cast most often.

 do I gain spell experience?

 time a spell is cast successfully, Drake gains experience points with that spell. (You
r get credit for "casting" a spell if you don't have enough mana.) Spell success is
rmined by the following criteria:

Spell	"Successful" means	Spell experience (SXP) gained			
Deadly Swarm	Causes damage to a foe	8	20	36	56
Firestorm	Causes damage to a foe	4	14	30	52
Holy Wrath	Causes damage to a foe	10	28	54	88
Lightning	Causes damage to a foe	5	20	45	88
Snap Freeze	Freezes at least one foe	6	16	30	48
Heroism	Spell is uninterrupted	6	22	48	84
Mana Shield	Spell is uninterrupted	4	22	54	100
Regeneration	Spell is uninterrupted	8	24	48	80

* Recasting this spell before its duration has run out does not gain additional
experience.

Spell Rank	Spell Experience Required
1	Find Spell
2	40
3	84
4	136
5	202

Specific effects of higher spell ranks are
included in each spell's description.

COMBAT

What's with all the colors and gems?

Nine realms of magic influence the world of Ardon. Four are Elemental: Earth, Air, Fire and Water. Three are Essential: Mind, Body and Spirit. Two are Ethereal: Light and Dark. When you fight, you're either using a normal attack or the power of one of the nine magical realms.

What are normal attacks?

A normal attack is any attack that uses a normal weapon (longsword, mace, ax, warhammer or exploding gem), unaided by magic.

What are magical attacks?

Any attack that uses magic is a magical attack. (We're in the School of the Obvious, here.) Spells are magical, of course, but you can also enchant any normal weapon so that its attack is magical.

How can I enchant my weapons?

There are nine kinds of magical weapon talismans, each associated with one of the realms of magic. If you attach one to your weapon, that weapon attacks with the magic of the talisman. For example, if you attach a Fire Weapon talisman ("Flamefang") to your longsword, you make Fire attacks, not normal attacks.

What difference does a Fire attack make?

Nearly all the creatures and other enemies you fight are aligned with one of the realms of magic. That makes them nearly immune to damage from that realm, but also makes them more susceptible to damage from an opposing realm. For example, a Fire sword (a longsword with a Fire Weapon talisman) can barely hurt a Lava Elemental, but a Frost sword will make short work of the same Elemental.

Which realms oppose each other?

Fire opposes Water.

Earth opposes Air.

Mind, Body and Spirit all oppose each other.

Light opposes Dark.

How much damage can I do?
Each weapon can do a certain amount of base damage. For example, a mace can do 25-55 points of normal damage. However, there are two important factors that change that base damage.

First, creatures that resist normal damage don't take as much damage from a mace. For example, no Elemental takes more than half damage from any normal attack. Each creature has at least some resistance to every kind of attack, whether normal or magical; many take no damage whatsoever from certain attacks unless you are very skilled.

Second, the stronger you are, and the more experienced you are, the more damage you can do. By the end of your adventure, you might be inflicting twice as much damage as when you started.

What about my armor — won't it protect me?
Absolutely — otherwise, why bother? The shield and armor descriptions (pp. 14-16) and list how much protection shields and armor give you.

Can I attack with my shield?
Again, absolutely. If you're a few steps away from your target, press ◎ + △ for a shield rush. This is particularly effective if you want to disrupt a spellcaster before he has a chance to finish his spell. Damage is based on how much stronger you are than your foe. And a spiked shield has an even better chance of damage and knockback.

Knockback? What's that?
Whenever you attack someone, there's a chance you knock him back, knocking him off-balance for a few seconds and disrupting any spells he might be casting. It's not long, but at least long enough to get off a quick strike or two. The harder you hit him, and the weaker he is, the greater the knockback. A spiked shield can increase knockback, as can several of your special attacks. (Of course, you can be knocked back also, so be alert for charging foes.)

You can't be knocked back if you're shield-rushing (◎ + △), and it's tough to knock you back while you're making a jumping attack (⊗, then □).

TIP

Be Aggressive

Crusaders of Might & Magic is a game that rewards aggression. Against most foes your best chance of survival is to wade right in and pound them as hard and fast as you possibly can. Save your shield moves and defensive tactics for special occasions ... for example, when trying to close with massed groups of missile-firing enemies.

Here's the formula for winning tough fights.

Make sure you have the right talisman equipped on your weapon.

1. Cast *Regeneration* before engaging any foe that looks like trouble.

2. Use your ranged spells first, to soften the enemy up. (Throwing weapons will do in a pinch, or against weak foes.)

3. Use Jumping attacks as much as possible. These are the only attacks you can execute while moving, and they give a 25% damage bonus when they hit.

4. Make sure you have your healing potions "in hand" and ready to use whenever you get a chance.

DRAKE

Can I knock someone back with my throwing axe or exploding gem?
Yes, but you have much less force behind a thrown weapon, so it's not nearly as likely.

What are the other special attacks?

▢	Well, first there's the **regular swing**. It does regular damage.
▢ + ◁	A **left swing** is just like a regular swing, except it specifies that you swing from right to left.
▢ + ▷	Ditto — a **right swing** swings from left to right.
▢, then △ + ▢	A **double swing**: first left, then right. This does the damage of two regular swings, but the total force of the two swings together is used to figure whether you knock back your foe. Note that this attack can be easy to interrupt, since it takes so long to complete.
▢ + △	An **overhead smash** takes longer, but inflicts 50% more damage.
▢,▢, then △ + ▢,▢	A **double overhead smash** (actually, an overhead smash immediately followed by an underhand return blow) is like a double swing — damage from each swing is figured separately, but the combined force determines the knockback. It, too, is easy to interrupt. In addition, a double overhead swing with a battle axe or warhammer has an even better chance of knockback.
▢ + ▽	A **180° reverse swing attack** swings your weapon up over your head, then continues with a downward smash at the area that was immediately behind you.
△, ▽, ▢ + △	A **180° reverse swing attack** swings your weapon up over your head, then continues with a downward smash at the area that was immediately behind you.
▢ + ✕ + △	A **charge** attack inflicts double damage and better knockback.

Is there any way to hit more than one foe with a single swing?
Actually, there are two ways — an overhead swing with a longsword or mace can hit multiple foes, as can a room cleaner with any weapon.

I'm in the middle of a great attack, when I realize I need to bail out and block

You can interrupt your own attack at anytime, by tapping or holding the shield block button (◎) and aborting to the appropriate shield maneuver instead — block or cover. Aborting to a shield maneuver is the *only* way that you can abort your attack once committed to it, until the attack is completed.

You can also interrupt a foe's more complicated attack with a shield block before he can finish it.

Hint

Special Attacks
The special attacks can be extremely useful. The tricky thing about them is the timing. They take much longer than a normal attack to execute, and if you're knocked back at all during your special attack, you lose whatever part of the attack you haven't yet completed. For example, the spin attack is particularly effective against tough foes ... if you can get it off.

DRAKE

Can I attack while I'm jumping?
Sure. Just jump (⊗), then swing (□). You can't make any of the special attacks during a jump, but it takes a vicious return attack to knock you back in the middle of a jump attack.

Why do Homunculi always run away when I'm about to win?
Because you're about to kill them. Wouldn't you run away? When a Homunculus has lost more than two-thirds of his Health, he decides whether to stick or run. Usually he runs. He's a lot more likely to run if *you* aren't as damaged as he is.

Can I hurt my allies with spells and exploding gems?
Fortunately, the magic powering your spells and gems is sophisticated enough not to hurt your allies. That is, as long as there's an enemy present. If you cast a spell or toss a gem while there are only friends present, the magic decides you *want* to hurt your allies, and obliges you. And your spells and gems can always knock back your allies (but not you).

TIP

Target Lock
Using Target Lock (R2) in close combat keeps you oriented towards your selected enemy. Whether or not you'll prefer to use the Target Lock probably depends on your personal fighting style. If you find it makes it easier for you to keep the enemy "in your sights," then use it. If you find it restricts your motion and limits your options, then don't.

HINT *Homunculi*

These hideous little annoyances deserve special attention. The thing you have to understand about Homunculi is that they *do not play fair*. They're designed to be as annoying as possible, while offering the bare minimum of reward. Therefore, they're the single exception to the "kill everything" rule that holds throughout the rest of the game. If you can blow past or evade Homunculi, than go ahead and do it ... they're not worth the frustration of trying to face them down.

They do have one useful function, if you have the mana for it, and that's training up your *Holy Wrath* spell. Sure, you're basically hunting chickens with a bazooka, but you don't have a lot of time game-wise to train up *Holy Wrath*, so it actually pays off in terms of experience to use it against some low-power enemies. Plus, Homunculi fry up *reeeal* good.

DRAKE

WEAPONS

Weapon	Damage	Cost (gold)
Battle Axe	44-96	350
Longsword	25-55	200
Mace	25-55	150
Warhammer	70-122	350
Throwing Axe	30-45	5
Exploding Gem	60-90	10

Exploding gems have Strength 30 for figuring knock-back. They affect all foes within a 20-foot radius.

If a longsword and mace do so much less damage, why would I ever want to use one?

Because you can swing a longsword or a mace much more quickly than you can a battle axe or warhammer. Sometimes their speed makes up for their reduced damage, especially if your special attacks keep getting disrupted before you can finish them, or enemy spellcasters keep getting their spells off before you can interrupt them with a strike.

Throwing Axe

Warhammer

Battle Axe

Mace

Longsword

DRAKE

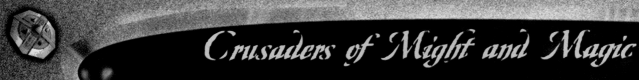

ARMOR

How good is my armor?

That depends on which armor you're wearing, and whether you're attacked with a normal or magical strike. (Remember, most attacks against you will be magical.) The amount of damage your armor absorbs is listed for each type of armor.

Armor	Against a Normal Attack	Against a Magical Attack	Cost (gold)
Leather	10%	none	Begin with it
Scale	20%	5%	500
Half-Plate	28%	10%	2200
Plate	36%	15%	5000
Black Guard	45%	20%	not for sale

Leather Armor

Scale Armor

DRAKE

Crusaders of Might and Magic

Half-Plate Armor

Plate Armor

Black Guard Armor

DRAKE

SHIELDS

DRAKE

How good is my shield?

All shields absorb 20% of any normal or Fire attack; they absorb 5% of any other magical attack. Of course, the attack has to be coming at your face (in your front 120° arc) — a shield can't help you unless it's between you and the attack, so shields are useless against attacks at your rear.

	Against a Normal or Fire Attack	Against other Magical Attacks	Cost (gold)
Shield	20%	5%	350

Spiked Shield

A spiked shield doubles shield rush damage.

Kite Shield

If you use a kite shield to shield block (◎), it doubles the shield's defense, as well as adding 50% more damage to any attack you make immediately after the shield block.

Tower Shield

A tower shield doubles your shield defense against all ranged attacks, including spells. This makes it very useful against casters.

What else can I do with my shield?

◎ + △	You can **shield rush**, an attack that can disrupt and knock back your opponent (see p. 9).
◎ (hold)	You can **cover** against an attack. Your shield stays in position until you release the ◎ button. Thus, you may try to minimize damage while waiting for an opening in an opponent's attack pattern.
◎ (tap)	You can attempt to **block** a melee strike. You've got to tap the ◎ button *after* your attacker starts his swing, but *before* he hits you. You can even block a shield rush, but you can't block spells or thrown weapons.

SPELLS

Fire Storm

This spell fires one to five fireballs (one per rank).

Either *Fire Storm* or *Lightning* can be your primary offensive spell, especially in the early going (whichever you prefer). Make this spell your routine start to any significant combat. Having a utilitarian combat spell at max by the end of the game is pretty much essential to success. Pick one to concentrate on, and stick with it until you've boosted it to rank 5, then work on improving your other spells, as well.

Rank	1	2	3	4	5
Mana Cost	20	35	50	65	80
Magical Realm	Fire				
Target	Where you point				
Damage	60-100/fireball				
Duration (secs.)	less than a second				
Radius (feet)	30				
Strength (knockback)	100				
Fire Resistance	Reduces the fireball damage				

Lightning

This spell sends a lightning bolt at your target(s). At rank 1, it will hit a single target. At each higher rank, it will arc off the first target and hit one more foe; if there aren't enough foes within the area, it will hit targets again.

Rank	1	2	3	4	5
Mana Cost	25	50	75	100	125
Magical Realm	Air				
Target	Where you point, plus nearby foes				
Damage	80-120/arc of lightning				
Duration (secs.)	less than a second				
Radius (feet)	–				
Strength (knockback)	50				
Air Resistance	Reduces the lightning damage				

DRAKE

Snap Freeze

This spell "freezes"" all foes within range. It causes no actual damage itself, but they can't move while frozen, making them much easier to attack.

Lots of foes have high Water resistance, reducing the duration of this spell, but it can still prove useful. In many cases, you just need to freeze your foes long enough for a quick strike or two, and most foes will stay frozen that long.

Beware of enemy mages who are ready and willing to *Snap Freeze* you, then hack your defenseless body into little pieces. It's not fun being on the receiving end. (Well, it's not fun for normal people.)

Rank	1	2	3	4	5
Mana Cost	30	40	50	60	70
Magical Realm	Water				
Target	Foes within a circle centered on you				
Damage Effect	Freezes foes in place				
Duration (secs.)	8	10	12	14	16
Radius (feet)	20	25	30	35	40
Strength (knockback)	–				
Water Resistance	Reduces the time frozen				

Deadly Swarm

This spell summons a swarm of insects that bite and sting all foes within range.

It's a good "fire and forget" spell, when you're ready to wade into combat. Cast it, then hack and slash to your heart's content. It's particularly useful against a coven of mages — each time it strikes one, his spell is disrupted, so you take far less damage while mowing them down.

On the other hand, you can't cast another spell while this one's active, so if spellcasting's your strength, stand back and repeatedly cast *Lighting* and *Fire Storm*, rather than *Deadly Swarm*.

Rank	1	2	3	4	5
Mana Cost	40	50	60	70	80
Magical Realm	Earth				
Target	Foes within a circle centered on you				
Damage	40-70/foe				
Duration (secs.)	6	9	12	15	18
Radius (feet)	15	20	25	30	35
Strength (knockback)	40	45	50	55	60
Earth Resistance	Reduces the stinging damage				

DRAKE

Mana Shield

This spell creates a magical field around your shield that increases your resistance to all magic, acting as "armor" against incoming spell damage. This spell may *not* be cast if you don't have a shield equipped.

Your regular armor protects against normal damage, and also provides a little protection from Fire damage. You want *Mana Shield* to protect against all the other realms of magic. This spell is only useful against spellcasters, but it is extremely valuable when a mage or shaman comes to call.

Rank	1	2	3	4	5
Mana Cost	20	55	90	125	160
Magical Realm	Mind				
Target	Yourself				
Effect	Blocks spells cast at you				
Your Spell Resistance	+10%	+20%	+30%	+40%	+50%
Duration (secs.)	40	45	50	55	60

Heroism

You summon up eldritch energies that imbue your body and spirit with increased energies. The result is an increase in your overall experience level. It does *not* increase weapon or spell ranks.

Regeneration is far more useful at the lower ranks and at lower experience levels, but take time to develop *Heroism*. At rank 1, it only boosts your experience level by 1, and there's little difference between (for instance) experience levels 2 and 3. However, at rank 5, this spell boosts your experience level by 5, and if you're already up to level 10 or 12, a boost to level 15 or 17 dramatically increases your damage, Health and Mana.

Rank	1	2	3	4	5
Mana Cost	30	55	80	105	130
Magical Realm	Spirit				
Target	Yourself				
Effect	Temporarily raises your experience by one level per rank (+1 to +5)				
Duration (secs.)	60				

DRAKE

Regeneration

This spell causes Drake's Health to regenerate at a rapid rate over time. The spell lasts for quite some time.

Simply *the* most useful, most important spell at the beginning of the game. *Regeneration* is often the edge you need to survive a tough battle. At higher experience levels, and higher ranks, *Heroism* and other spells are just as useful.

Rank	1	2	3	4	5
Mana Cost	40	60	80	100	120
Magical Realm	Body				
Target	Yourself				
Effect	Restores 5 Health per second				
Duration (secs.)	30	35	40	45	50

Holy Wrath

This spell strikes all foes around you, but especially wreaks havoc with most undead, who are vulnerable to Light damage.

This powerful spell offers a unique challenge, because it doesn't show up until well into the game. It also costs a lot of mana to cast it. However, if you can manage your mana supply so that you can afford to make this spell a regular part of your combat routine, it will really pay off. There is probably nothing that will do more to ease your journey through the last couple of quests than having *Holy Wrath* at max level or close to it, especially with its hyped-up damage to undead.

Rank	1	2	3	4	5
Mana Cost	50	70	90	110	130
Magical Realm	Light				
Target	Foes within a circle centered on you				
Damage Effect	100-150/foe				
Duration (secs.)	.5	.75	1.0	1.25	1.5
Radius (feet)	15	20	25	30	35
Strength (knockback)	100				

TIP

Opposing Spells and Talismans

Finding talismans is an important part of developing your character ... just as important as increasing your experience levels through combat.

There are a total of 27 talismans in the game ... one weapon, shield and armor talisman for each of the nine magical realms. You can find them all during your adventures (although some are very well hidden, and you might miss them), and you can also buy most of the talismans at the three shops in the game. You should be prepared to do whatever it takes to get a full set of talismans by the time you reach the end of the game.

There are also eight spells available to Drake, and like the talismans they can be either found during an adventure or bought from a merchant. While you should concentrate most of your energies on developing certain key spells (see **Character Development**, p. 5), you'll certainly want to acquire a full set of spells, and be acquainted with what they can do for you.

Shield and armor talismans each increase your resistance against a certain realm of magic, and those creatures attacking with the magic of that realm, and they are equipped automatically. That is, once you find a shield or armor talisman, its benefit is yours forever. Weapon talismans, however, have to be specifically selected and applied to your weapon. Once you find a weapon talisman, you'll always have it with you, but you won't get any benefit from it while it's not attached to your weapon.

Always try to hit a foe with the spells and talismans that he resists the least.

This rule is so basic to the whole game that it almost doesn't need to be said, but it's so important that it can't be ignored.

If you hit a foe with a spell or a weapon talisman aligned with the realm that opposes it you do significantly more damage, but if you hit it with the magic of its own realm, you do a great deal less damage. Therefore, it pays — in fact it's pretty essential — to know which realms oppose one another, and in which realm each foe is most vulnerable.

DRAKE

TALISMANS

What does a talisman do?

If you attach a weapon talisman to a weapon, all damage you inflict with that weapon is doubled and becomes magical damage. For example, if you bind a Mind Weapon talisman (Razor's Edge) on your longsword, your longsword inflicts 44-100 points of Mind damage (useful against most Dashers and those undead who have lower resistances to Mind damage).

If you attach a shield or armor talisman to your shield or armor, *you* have increased resistance against that type of magic. For example, an Air Shield talisman (the Lightning Rune) gives you an additional 10% resistance against Lightning and other Air attacks. Every armor talisman gives you 20% more resistance to its realm of magic; every shield talisman gives you 10% more resistance to its realm of magic.

Armor Talisman

How do I get them?

Mostly, you find them. You can buy some of them from merchants, but they're expensive — you've got to give both gems (of the appropriate type) and gold to get any talisman. Light and Dark talismans aren't for sale.

Shield Talisman

Why would I want more than three talismans — one each for my weapon, armor and shield?

Because you can switch between them — you can equip your Fire Weapon talisman against a Yeti, then switch it for your Air Weapon talisman against Stone Elementals. Meanwhile, your Water Shield and Armor talismans are protecting you against the Yeti's attack, while your Earth Shield and Armor talismans protect you against the Stone Elementals.

Can I put more than one talisman on my weapon?

No, you can only have one talisman on a weapon at a time. (You can also have one shield talisman and one armor talisman equipped at the same time.) However, you can freely switch all your talismans to better prepare for each new foe.

Weapon Talisman

Common Name	Specific Name	Cost	Where first found
Air Armor	Talisman of Storms	1100 + 7 gems	Glaciers (City of Anc.)
Earth Armor	Barkskin Talisman	1100 + 7 gems	Corantha (Rebellion)
Fire Armor	Flame Talisman	1100 + 7 gems	Corantha (Scepter)
Water Armor	Glacial Talisman	1100 + 7 gems	Corantha (Elemental Scourge)
Body Armor	Sinew Talisman	1100 + 7 gems	Duskwood (Thunder Clan)
Mind Armor	Ohkam's Talisman	1100 + 7 gems	Citadel (Second Visit)
Spirit Armor	Karmic Talisman	1100 + 7 gems	Glaciers (Ships' Gr.)
Light Armor	Talisman of Teruvia	not for sale	Glaciers (City of Anc.)
Dark Armor	Talisman of Doom	not for sale	Duskwood (Grub Hive)
Air Shield	Lightning Rune	600 + 3 gems	Escape from Stronghold
Earth Shield	Rune of Ash	600 + 3 gems	Corantha (Rebellion)
Fire Shield	Hellforge Rune	600 + 3 gems	Corantha (First Visit)
Water Shield	Rune of the Deeps	600 + 3 gems	Duskwood (Thunder Clan)
Body Shield	Blood Rune	600 + 3 gems	Dasher Village
Mind Shield	Rune of Clarity	600 + 3 gems	Duskwood (Djad)
Spirit Shield	Astral Rune	600 + 3 gems	Glaciers (City of Anc.)
Light Shield.	Rune of Sepallia	not for sale	Citadel (Second Visit)
Dark Shield	Rune of Shadow	not for sale	Stronghold (Behind L)
Air Weapon	Thundermaker	1500 + 10 gems	Citadel (Second Visit)
Earth Weapon	Oakheart	1500 + 10 gems	Duskwood (Djad)
Fire Weapon	Flamefang	1500 + 10 gems	Corantha (Elemental Scourge)
Water Weapon	Ice Claw	1500 + 10 gems	Corantha (Rebellion)
Body Weapon	Bonemender *	1900 + 10 gems	Duskwood (Djad)
Mind Weapon	Razor's Edge *	1900 + 10 gems	Stronghold (Behind L)
Spirit Weapon	Soul Bastion *	2100 + 10 gems	Dasher Village
Light Weapon	Star of Erathia	not for sale	Glaciers (Ships' Gr.)
Dark Weapon	Nightbringer	not for sale	Corantha (Elemental Scourge)

* Bonemender gives you a 20% Health boost while it is equipped, and Razor's Edge gives you a 20% Mana boost. Soul Bastion gives you a 10% boost to both Health and Mana while it is equipped.

HINT What's the best way to use the gold you find lying around?

The most basic use for cash is to keep your enough potions on hand. But if you're spending all or most of your gold on potions, you probably need to go back and work on your combat fundamentals some more.

Your major expense is probably getting your armor up to max. Everything else in the game you can find for free, if you search with reasonable care, but the very best armor has to be purchased.

While all the talismans and spells are there to be found, you might miss one or two, in which case you should definitely buy any you missed before the endgame, if it's available.

DRAKE

OTHER GOODIES

How effective is Vanish Dust?

A foe can "see" (detect) you at a much greater range if you're in front of him (a 120° arc for the mathematicians among us). If you're to his side or behind him, you can get much closer before he realizes you're there. Vanish Dust doesn't exactly make you vanish, but it does let you come as close to a foe's face as to his back before he realizes you're there. Note that few foes will actually let you walk up and swing at them before they notice you.

Vanish Dust doesn't make you completely invisible. Instead, it greatly reduces the range at which enemy creatures can detect your presence. Avoiding fights is not recommended as a general policy (see **Be Aggressive**, p. 9), but there are times when it's desirable — basically, when the enemy is tough, you're short on Healing potions, and the nearest Save Point is far off. When you use Vanish Dust to evade combat, make sure you move around each enemy in a long, curved arc, to stay well outside of his detection range.

Item	Cost (gold)	Effect
Healing Potion	*25*	*Restores all lost Health*
Mana Potion	*25*	*Restores all lost Mana*
Restore Potion	*40*	*Restores all lost Health and Mana*
Vanish Dust	*25*	*Significantly reduces foe's ability to detect you; lasts 30 seconds*
Dasher Nut	*40*	*Lets you run faster and jump higher; lasts 30 seconds*

Mana Potion

Restore Potion

Dasher Nut

Healing Potion

Vanishing Dust

TIP

Dasher Nuts make you faster. You may find this useful in combat, or you may not. They can be useful in evasion — just zip right past that room full of monsters or that *Lightning* trap. Their most definite advantage is in helping you jump up to reach concealed treasure troves, which would be much harder (perhaps impossible) to reach without a Dasher Nut boost.

⌐RCHANTS

⌐ three merchant shops in the game. One is in Citadel, run by the Quartermaster
⌐ One is in Corantha, run by the twin smiths Castor and Pollux. The third is in
⌐er village, run by T'Pok. Their prices never vary, and are listed with the various
⌐tem descriptions in this book.

	Price	Citadel Korinda	Corantha Castor/Pollux	Dasher T'Pok
Scale Armor	500	Yes	Yes	
Half-Plate Armor	2200	Yes	Yes	
Plate Armor	5000	Yes	Yes	
Kite Shield	350	Yes		
Tower Shield	350		Yes	
Healing Potion	25	Yes	Yes	Yes
Mana Potion	25	Yes	Yes	Yes
Restore Potion	40	Yes	Yes	Yes
Throwing Axe	5	Yes	Yes	Yes
Exploding Gem	10	Yes	Yes	Yes
Dasher Nut	40			Yes
Vanish Dust	25			Yes
All Air Talismans	below		Yes	
All Earth Talismans	below		Yes	
All Fire Talismans	below		Yes	
All Water Talismans	below		Yes	
All Body Talismans	below	Yes		
All Mind Talismans	below	Yes		
All Spirit Talismans	below			Yes

All Armor talismans cost 1100 gold and 7 gems of the appropriate realm.

All Shield talismans cost 600 gold and 3 gems of the appropriate realm.

Most Weapon talismans cost 1500 gold and 10 gems of the appropriate realm.

Body and Mind Weapon talismans cost 1900 gold and 10 body or mind gems.

A Spirit Weapon talisman costs 2100 gold and 10 spirit gems.

DRAKE

Celestia, The Lady Archon

Dear Nomandi,

I can't tell you how thrilled I was to get your letter after all these years. Truthfully, most of us had thought you were long since dead, and I'm delighted to find how mistaken we were. You'll understand if this note is a bit rushed, as I have to hurry to get it back to your "messenger" before it departs.

Time is short, so I'll begin with a confession. Over the years, I've come around closer and closer to your opinion on the question of Celestia. These days the commander, frankly, unnerves me. Mind you, I have no evidence that would warrant formal charges. Taken individually, each of her decisions makes perfect sense, and in general the Order seems to go on with considerable efficiency, and even some success against the Legion. On another level, however, this is not the noble Order that you and I joined so many years ago. Maybe I'm just an old man too tired to change with the times, but these new recruits, this "High Guard," are not Crusaders as I understand the word. They're more like mercenaries, brash and cold blooded.

As for Celestia herself, there are just so many questions. How old is that woman? I remember when she, you and I were all young officers. Today she does not look like a young woman, but she doesn't look nearly as old as I do, or even as you did when you left us years ago. Even in the early days she always kept her past mysterious.

Here's what I think bothers me the most. When you and I began in the Order, the Crusaders were based on ideals. Oh, surely there were some unpleasant decisions that had to be made in battle, but the command was still capable of occasionally doing something just because it was the right thing to do, even if it came at a cost. In all these years of her command, I have never ... never once ... seen Celestia do anything that did not carry a clear tactical advantage. She will cheerfully give over a whole town to the Legion if she thinks our forces can more efficiently be deployed elsewhere. Oh, all of her decisions make sense, her logic is always inassailable, but I've never seen any sign that such decisions tear at her heart, or even that she has one. I tell you, Nomandi, I am certain that at least twice the only thing that kept her from ordering the Crusaders themselves to destroy a town and slaughter its civilians (to keep them from going to the Legion) was the certainty that the Old Guard would have risen up against her. She still needs us, but there are fewer of us every year.

Such dark thoughts, and time flies. I would like to end on a cheerier note, but I must get this missive to the messenger if it has any hope of reaching you. Try to get me another letter soon, old friend, and I promise to have a longer and (at least somewhat) less gloomy letter ready for you when it gets here.

Your brother in arms,

Steggan, Knight

Health	720
Strength	54
Resistances (%)	100 all
Spells Deadly Swarm (3), Firestorm (3)	
Attacks	Fist (25-45) (Spirit)
Damage Bonus (%)	+50 Melee
	+10 Ranged

Chamber Guardians

Health	500
Strength	60
Resistances (%)	100 Normal / Spirit
	85 Fire / Earth / Air / Water
	85 Body / Mind / Light / Dark
Attacks	Fist (25-45) (Light)
Damage Bonus (%)	+60 Melee
	+10 Ranged
Spells Lightning (2), Deadly Swarm (2)	

Aerrin

Dear Daddy,

I'm so excited, they've given me my own boat!

It's small, of course. Just a pinnace. I'm the only crew she needs. She's old, but steady. I call her the Sparrow. I mostly make the run from Citadel to our Stronghold forces, but sometimes I get to take her out on longer jaunts, taking knights for special missions behind the lines and such.

I know she's nothing like the great ships you used to pilot, with their weapons and cargo and crew, but after all this is just my first command. Good navigators are in short supply these days, and everyone says that once I prove myself reliable it's only a matter of time. I do worry though ... the fighting is so intense, and we've lost so many warships over the last few years. Sometimes I wonder if there'll be any left when I'm ready.

I've flown Celestia twice now, once to meet with some Dwarves about some Citadel business. She asked my name and knew me for your daughter. The second time was to allow her to observe a battle near the borders of Duskwood. That flight was the closest I've ever been to a great battle, and I'm not ashamed to admit I was ter-rified. Especially when Celestia told me to go down within 100 feet of some very intense fighting. There was a whole knot of Legion mages on this little hill, and they started casting lightning bolts at us at a furious pace. They couldn't reach us, but they boiled the air horribly. I kept the keel steady though, and when we finally withdrew Celestia thanked me for my handling.

I've been so busy with the Sparrow that I've had little time for my other studies, but I still hope to be a real Crusader soon. The fighting's been so heavy that they haven't had time to test many new candidates lately, but I expect they'll have to soon, because casualties have been heavy as well. I'm not sure if I'll make it in the next batch, though. They need me where I am (I told you how short they were on good pilots), but this would be an unseemly posting for a true knight. I might have to wait until one of the great galleons is desperate for a junior officer.

Some of the knights like to flirt with me, but I still haven't found that special one. I'm not sure if I'd want to marry a knight anyway. Two knights in one household sounds like one too many, don't you think? Maybe a craftsman will be more to my taste, or perhaps a minstrel ... we could travel together. Of course, maybe I'll meet a real hero who'll sweep me off my feet in uncontrollable passion! (I'm just kidding.)

Oh Daddy, I really wish you were still alive, so we could sail together and talk like we used to. But it helps so much to write to you like this, I really feel that you're reading every word I write. Are you? If only you could write back.

I have to go now, it's time for the weekly supply run.

Your Loving Daughter,

Aerrin

Health	700
Strength	36
Resistances (%)	100 all
Spells	Lightning (2)
	Heroism (4)
Attacks	Fist (25-45)
Damage Bonus (%)	+20 Melee
	+10 Ranged

FRIENDS & FOES

Ursan, Captain of the Crusade

Captain Ursan,

You place me in a difficult position, captain. I am not accustomed to tolerating insubordination from my field commanders, however I also do not wish to taint the undeniable heroism of your recent actions with a public reprimand. Thus, this letter. I intend to make my wishes known with the greatest possible clarity, and I can assure you that any further failure to obey my orders or my policies will be met with a far more firm response.

Commanders, Captain, command units in the field. They do not go rushing off on ill-considered, impromptu "secret missions." I do not care how important the mission was, and I do not care how well qualified you might be for it. You have good men under your command, and one of their duties is to undertake risky missions. If there's a messy job that needs to be done, order someone to do it, or find a volunteer.

Believe me, Captain, nobody understands better than I your desire to take the brunt of the fighting on your own shoulders. I'm a field commander by nature, but I've spent the last 10 years floating up here in this cloud castle while countless good Crusaders have died below. It breaks my heart every time a battle takes place down there while I'm up here, but here is where I stay, because here is where I'm needed.

So I completely understand your desire not to commit the men to any mission you would not undertake yourself, but I assure you, your courage is not in question. It's the men whom you endanger most when you undertake one of these adventures. What would have become of your unit if you had not returned? Would they have been able to hold three days in the pass without you there with them? I will grant you that this time your gamble paid off rather spectacularly, but I cannot allow my commanders to gamble with their own lives. War is chancy enough as it is. A chess master never risks a queen when he can use a knight, and never risks a knight when a pawn will serve. Even if you have to expend a half dozen men or more to accomplish the mission, that's preferable to risking yourself. That's distasteful, but it's nonetheless true.

There could be great things in your future, Captain. I'm not a young woman, and I won't be commanding the Order forever. You have many of the qualities of foresight, initiative and experience that the Crusaders need at the highest levels. It will not be possible, however, to give any serious consideration to your further advancement until you have demonstrated an ability to take your obligations seriously at your present level.

Therefore, I am ordering you to report to me at Citadel, immediately. I believe that a nice long assignment as the chief of my staff will serve admirably, both as a "reward" for your heroism and as "punishment" for your recklessness.

Yrs.

Celestia, Commander, Order of Crusaders

Health	1000
Strength	60
Resistances (%)	100 all
Attacks	Longsword Throwing Axe (Light)
Damage Bonus (%)	+60 Melee +10 Ranged
Shield	Crusader

FRIENDS & FOES

Old Guard Crusader

Health	700
Strength	36
Resistances (%)	60 Normal
	41 Body
	40 Fire / Earth / Air / Water
	40 Spirit / Mind / Light / Dark
Attacks	Longsword
	Throwing Axe
Damage Bonus (%)	+20 Melee
	+10 Ranged
Shield	Tower

High Guard Crusader

Health	650
Strength	36
Resistances (%)	70 Normal
	56 Body
	55 Fire / Earth / Air / Water
	55 Spirit / Mind / Light / Dark
Attacks	Longsword
Damage Bonus (%)	+20 Melee
	+10 Ranged
Shield	Crusader

Korinda, Crusader Quartermaster

Health	340
Strength	36
Resistances (%)	80 Normal
	76 Air
	75 Fire / Earth / Water / Body
	75 Spirit / Mind / Light / Dark
Spells	Deadly Swarm (4)
Attacks	Fist (25-45)
Damage Bonus (%)	+20 Melee
	+10 Ranged

FRIENDS & FOES

Tamris, Dasher Chieftain

Commander,

Here, as you ordered, is my report on Tamris and the Dashers.

As you know, as an infant I was left a foundling in the Duskwood, when my parents were slain by a Legion ambush. I was adopted by the Dashers and raised in the house of Tamris.

Since I returned to my own people, I have met many folk who think the Dashers are primitives. That's a mistake. Dashers live their lives according to a principle that we usually translate as "efficiency," because it involves making use only of what's necessary, and then using it to its fullest. But the word also means something like "simplicity," and something like "purity." The point is that the Dashers don't live off the land because they're not smart enough to farm or build as humans do, but because they're smart enough not to need to farm or build.

Take books, for example. I've heard many folk call the Dashers illiterate. It's true that they don't write things down, but you also have to know that even a half-grown Dasher child knows the "17 Great Stories" by heart and word for word. Each of the stories takes at least two or three hours to sing. By the time he's ready to be acknowledged an adult, he must know upwards of a hundred, and the elders (Dashers usually live at least two hundred years, barring mishap) can know thousands. An elder Dasher has all the information of a great library right there in his head, so it's no wonder he has no time for books.

As for Tamris, he was my foster father, but he was more like a big brother. When I was a boy, he was about 50, I think, which is very young for a Dasher war-leader. That would make him less than 70 today, which is an unheard-of age for a High Chief.

Tamris likes humans, which is unusual in a Dasher. I think he was really thrilled to have a human child (me, that is) to live in his house and watch him grow up. He was always most kind and attentive to my needs, and I loved to spend time with him. Most Dashers hold humans pretty much in contempt. They call us "complicated," and "disorganized" (which are pretty big put-downs to a Dasher). Tamris, while as proud of the Dasher way as anybody (he has more lore already than many Dashers three times his age), sees our way as not so much inferior as different. He thinks he can learn from us, which is very forward-thinking for a Dasher.

By your leave, Commander, I was told to include my opinions, and I'll speak plainly. I believe that the Dashers could be very valuable allies of the Order. They hate undead and would welcome a chance to mobilize against Necros. It is very important, however, that the Crusaders treat the Dashers as equals. If we try to approach them as their betters (which humans have always been wont to do, there are many stories about it) they'll refuse to even talk to us.

Respectfully,

Dikken, Knight and Scout

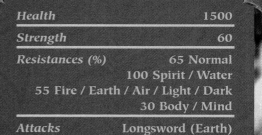

Health	1500
Strength	60
Resistances (%)	65 Normal
	100 Spirit / Water
	55 Fire / Earth / Air / Light / Dark
	30 Body / Mind
Attacks	Longsword (Earth)
Damage Bonus (%)	+110 Melee
	+60 Ranged

Dasher Ranger

Level / XP Value	5 / 2500
Health	450
Strength	60
Resistances (%)	100 Spirit
	65 Normal
	65 Fire / Earth / Air / Water
	65 Light / Dark
	40 Body / Mind
Spells	Deadly Swarm (1)
	Heroism (1)
Attacks	Longsword (Body)
Damage Bonus (%)	+110 Melee
	+60 Ranged

Dasher Scout

Level / XP Value	3 / 900
Health	300
Strength	50
Resistances (%)	100 Spirit
	45 Normal, 20 Body / Mind
	40 Fire / Earth / Air / Water
	40 Light / Dark
Attacks	Short Axe
	Throwing Axe
Damage Bonus (%)	+90 Melee
	+60 Ranged

Dasher Brute

Level / XP Value	4 / 1600
Health	400
Strength	60
Resistances (%)	100 Spirit
	60 Fire / Earth / Air / Water
	60 Light / Dark, 55 Normal
	40 Body / Mind
Attacks	Club
Damage Bonus (%)	+60 Melee
	+10 Ranged
Shield	Spiked

Dwarven Stonehearts

Lady Celestia,

Tonight marks my third week here in Corantha, and I am starting to get some feeling, I believe, for the situation among the Dwarves.

I have met several times with Dain, the crown prince (King Aiden customarily allows his son to represent him in routine diplomatic matters). We get on very well together, and Dain himself has told me that he desires to continue and strengthen the Dwarven/Crusader alliance. Furthermore, Dain is an intelligent and resolute Dwarf, greatly loved by his people, or at least the influential clan Dwarves of the cities.

That's the good news.

And there's the bad news. There's growing unrest among the Ironpick caste of the lower mines. As far as I can tell, it's only a small movement of radicals at the moment, but the tide of dissent seems to be growing. To some extent this feeling among the Ironpick is justified, as they have been disenfranchised for generations, despite being the very cornerstone of Dwarven prosperity with their work in the mines.

However there is also about the situation a distinct odour of outside agitation. To some extent this seems to be the work of Dain's brother, Tor, who covets power, despite the fact that Aiden continues to allow Tor to retain his seat on the High Council. At this time I do not know if the Legion is also actively encouraging the Ironpick rebels ... the possibility cannot be ruled out.

My overall assessment of the situation at the moment is that it is both stable and fragile. I believe Aiden can keep the forces of rebellion in hand. The greatest danger is that the king would somehow be removed from the picture, through mishap, abduction or assassination. If that were to happen the situation would certainly destabilize rapidly. I have advised Dain to strengthen the personal security of the royal family, and even offered him the services of Crusader guards (pending your approval, of course). He has taken the first suggestion under advisement, but utterly rejected the second. Under the Dwarven "Rule of Strength," it is appropriate that the regent be well guarded, but only by loyal Dwarves. We humans remain outsiders.

I shall continue to keep you appraised of the situation as my understanding evolves.

With profound respect,

Drammar, Knight and Counselor

DAIN

Health	750
Strength	55
Resistances (%)	100 all
Attacks	Warhammer (Mind)
Damage Bonus (%)	+100 Melee
	+60 Ranged
Shield	Tower

TOR

Health	680
Strength	55
Resistances (%)	100 all
Attacks	Short Axe
Damage Bonus (%)	+100 Melee
	+60 Ranged
Spells	Deadly Swarm (1)
	Regeneration (1)

Stoneheart Regular

Level / XP Value	1 / 100
Health	400
Strength	55
Resistances (%)	100 Earth
	65 Fire / Water / Body / Spirit
	65 Mind / Light / Dark
	60 Normal, 45 Air
Attacks	Warhammer
Throwing Axe	
Damage Bonus (%)	+100 Melee
	+60 Ranged
Shield	Tower

Castor & Pollux, Dwarven Smithies

Health	700
Strength	55
Resistances (%)	100 Earth
	65 Fire / Water / Body / Spirit
	65 Mind / Light / Dark
	60 Normal, 45 Air
Attacks	Short Axe
	Exploding Gem
Damage Bonus (%)	+100 Melee
	+60 Ranged
Shield	Crusader

General Martel, Warlord of Corantha

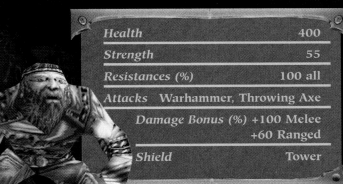

Health	400
Strength	55
Resistances (%)	100 all
Attacks	Warhammer, Throwing Axe
Damage Bonus (%)	+100 Melee
	+60 Ranged
Shield	Tower

King Aiden Stoneheart

Level / XP Value	8 / 6400
Health	1500
Strength	60
Resistances (%)	85 Normal
	100 Water / Body / Dark
	65 Fire / Earth / Air / Spirit
	50 Mind / Light
Spells	Holy Wrath (2)
Attacks	Warhammer (Dark)
Damage Bonus (%)	+60 Melee
	+10 Range

FRIENDS & FOES

Ironpick Rebel

Level / XP Value	2 / 400
Health	300
Strength	45
Resistances (%)	80 Mind
	60 Normal, 30 Body
	50 Fire / Earth / Air / Water
	50 Spirit / Light / Dark
Attacks	Short Axe or Mace
	Throwing Axe
Damage Bonus (%)	+30 Melee
	+10 Ranged
Shield	Spiked

Ironpick Mage

Level / XP Value	4 / 1600
Health	250
Strength	40
Resistances (%)	80 Mind
55 Fire / Earth / Air / Water / Light / Dark	
	40 Normal, 35 Body
Spells	Lightning (1)
	Firestorm (1), Regeneration (2)
Attacks	Fist (25-45)
Damage Bonus (%)	+20 Melee
	+10 Ranged

Ironpick Zealot

Level / XP Value	3 / 900
Health	200
Strength	50
Resistances (%)	90 Mind
	50 Normal, 25 Body
	45 Fire / Earth / Air / Water
	45 Spirit / Light / Dark
Attacks	Fist (30-60)
	Exploding Gem
Damage Bonus (%)	+60 Melee
	+30 Ranged

eeeeeeeeee
Prima's Official Strategy Guide

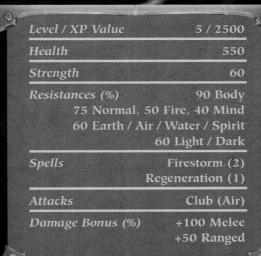

Ogre Shaman

Level / XP Value	5 / 2500
Health	550
Strength	60
Resistances (%)	90 Body
	75 Normal, 50 Fire, 40 Mind
	60 Earth / Air / Water / Spirit
	60 Light / Dark
Spells	Firestorm (2)
	Regeneration (1)
Attacks	Club (Air)
Damage Bonus (%)	+100 Melee
	+50 Ranged

Ogre Clansman

Level / XP Value	3 / 900
Health	500
Strength	65
Resistances (%)	90 Body
	75 Normal, 50 Fire, 40 Mind
	60 Earth / Air / Water / Spirit
	60 Light / Dark
Attacks	Club
Damage Bonus (%)	+100 Melee
	+50 Ranged

Ogre Clan Leader

Level / XP Value	9 / 8100
Health	1500
Strength	80
Resistances (%)	90 Body
	80 Normal, 50 Fire, 45 Mind
	60 Earth / Air / Water / Spirit
	60 Light / Dark
Attacks	Battle Axe (Earth)
Damage Bonus (%)	+140 Melee
	+60 Ranged
Spells	Deadly Swarm (2)
	Regeneration (3)

Grub Queen

PROPOSAL FOR SUPPLY LINE HEADQUARTERS

TO: Necros, the great leader of the Legion

Your Supreme Darkness,

I must admit that your request to relocate the supply lifeline of our Legion troops came at a most difficult time, but is a stroke of genius. I am, as always, greatly indebted for this responsibility under your tutelage. After a great many hours of thought, I have constructed a plan I believe will please you.

The solution came to me in a vision, a dream in which I was captured by a band of idiotic Ogres armed only with spears and Light talismans. They bound me tightly to the entrance of an out-of-the-way cave for two courses of the sun and moon. During my imagined imprisonment, I dreamt — if one can dream within a nightmare — that a small band of creatures arrived, chanting a dark melody as they freed me. Upon awakening in my own bunk, I immediately recorded my vision and set out to locate an appropriate underground cave close to all fronts of battle.

Several Ogre scouts led me to a well-hidden entrance on the edge of Duskwood, where I discovered the Grubs. These weak, tiny creatures live in a hive and appear to be completely loyal to their royal leader. A fearsome spectacle, the Grub Queen stands at ten times my height and possesses multiple powers of physical attack — spittles of fire, poison mandibles and razor-sharp appendages. Though quite hostile at our first meeting, the Queen Grub appears relatively neutral to our cause and content to let us use her kingdom for a small fee.

As requested, I have drawn up detailed plans for this underground supply line and will deliver them by courier for approval.

Yours in loyalty,

-Scimmilon, Legion Supply Commander

Hive Warrior

Level / XP Value	6 / 3600
Health	700
Strength	60
Resistances (%)	75 Normal
	100 Body attacks
	70 Fire / Earth / Air / Water
	70 Spirit / Light / Dark
	50 Mind
Attacks	Fist (30-60)
Damage Bonus (%)	+60 Melee
	+10 Ranged

Revenant Crewman, Captain

Level / XP Value	7 / 4900
Health	600
Strength	70
Resistances (%)	100 Normal
	100 Water / Spirit
	65 Fire / Earth / Air / Light
	50 Body / Mind / Dark
Attacks	Longsword
Damage Bonus (%)	+70 Melee
	+10 Ranged
Shield	Kite

Level / XP Value	10 / 10000
Health	1500
Strength	42
Resistances (%)	100 Normal
	100 Normal / Water / Spirit
	65 Fire / Earth / Air / Light
	50 Body / Mind / Dark
Spells	Holy Wrath (2)
Attacks	Longsword (Light)
Damage Bonus (%)	+30 Melee
	+10 Ranged
Shield	Kite

FRIENDS & FOES

Lava Elemental

Level / XP Value	6 / 3600
Health	400
Strength	60
Resistances (%)	100 Fire
70 Earth, 60 Normal, 50 Air, 35 Water	
55 Body / Spirit / Mind / Light / Dark	
Spells	Firestorm (2)
Attacks	Fist (30-60) (Fire)
Damage Bonus (%)	+60 Melee
	+10 Ranged

Glacier Elemental

Level / XP Value	6 / 3600
Health	700
Strength	85
Resistances (%)	100 Water
70 Normal, 70 Earth / Air, 40 Fire	
60 Body / Spirit / Mind / Light / Dark	
Spells	Snap Freeze (2)
Attacks	Fist (35-80) (Water)
Damage Bonus (%)	+100 Melee
	+10 Ranged

Stone Elemental, Elemental Lord

Level / XP Value	10 / 10000
Health	2500
Strength	85
Resistances (%)	80 Fire / Water, 40 Air
	100 Earth, 70 Normal
65 Body / Spirit / Mind / Light / Dark	
Spells	Regeneration (3)
Attacks	Fist (35-80) (Body)
Damage Bonus (%)	+100 Melee
	+10 Ranged

Level / XP Value	5 / 2500
Health	400
Strength	65
Resistances (%)	100 Earth
65 Normal, 70 Fire, 50 Water / Body	
60 Spirit / Mind / Light / Dark, 35 Air	
Attacks	Fist (30-60)
Damage Bonus (%)	+60 Melee
	+10 Ranged

Ice Elemental

Level / XP Value	5 / 2500
Health	400
Strength	60
Resistances (%)	100 Water
	70 Normal / Earth / Air, 40 Fire
	60 Body / Spirit / Mind / Light / Dark
Attacks	Fist (30-60)
Damage Bonus (%)	+60 Melee
	+10 Ranged

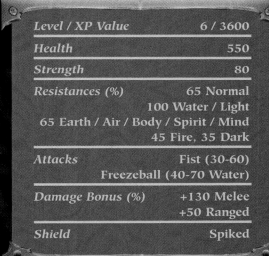

Yeti

Level / XP Value	6 / 3600
Health	550
Strength	80
Resistances (%)	65 Normal
	100 Water / Light
	65 Earth / Air / Body / Spirit / Mind
	45 Fire, 35 Dark
Attacks	Fist (30-60)
	Freezeball (40-70 Water)
Damage Bonus (%)	+130 Melee
	+50 Ranged
Shield	Spiked

Yeti Lord

Level / XP Value	9 / 8100
Health	2000
Strength	100
Resistances (%)	75 Normal, 55 Fire,
	100 Water / Light, 45 Dark
	70 Earth / Air / Body / Spirit / Mind
Attacks	Fist (30-60) (Light)
Damage Bonus (%)	+160 Melee
	+50 Ranged
Spells	Holy Wrath (3)
	Regeneration (2)

Yeti Shaman

Level / XP Value	7 / 4900
Health	600
Strength	80
Resistances (%)	70 Normal, 50 Fire
	100 Water / Light, 40 Dark
	70 Earth / Air / Body / Spirit / Mind
Spells	Holy Wrath (2)
Attacks	Fist (30-60) (Water)
Damage Bonus (%)	+130 Melee
	+50 Ranged

FRIENDS & FOES

Black Guard Sentry

To all unit commanders

From Crusader High Command

Due to the growing tide of rumor in the ranks about the nature of our enemy, we are issuing this document, which records some of the known facts about the Legion. It is possible that the facts as we know them may be more damaging to morale than wild rumor, so disseminate this knowledge with caution.

The troops of the Legion of the Fallen are reanimated corpses of fallen humans. Any corpse can be converted into an animate skeleton, but the Legion prefers to "recruit" from those who had martial skills in life, as this produces a more formidable warrior.

There are two known methods for creating a skeleton warrior. The first is a rather complicated necromantic ritual, which has been known to wizards for centuries, and which can only work on one corpse at a time. The second is unique to the Legion. It appears that undead spell casters in the presence of a large concentration of other undead (i.e., a Legion army), can call upon the collective unnatural "vitality" of the assembled hosts and inflict their condition on any reasonably intact corpse within a radius of several miles. (The exact radius is determined by the number of casters and the available pool of undead.) This is how the Legion is able to accomplish their most terrifying feat, the animation of recently slain enemies.

When a skeleton is newly raised, it is able to do little except mechanically follow orders. As time goes by, however, it begins to regain memories of life. At this point a few Legionnaires turn renegade, as former loyalties reassert themselves. Such rogue Legionnaires are put down as soon as they're detected. Most, however, remain loyal to the Legion. This is because the undead warrior harbors an intense desire to return to full life. It remembers the pleasures of vitality, but cannot experience them, which is a source of torment. Yet it cannot bear the thought of laying down its last shards of living sensation.

The Legion are taught that, once their conquest is complete, Necros will have the resources necessary to return them all to full life once more. This promise is sufficient to keep most warriors of the Legion in servitude. How much of this loyalty is a magical glamour cast on the minds of the Legionnaires, and how much is simple persuasion, is a matter of some conjecture.

Level / XP Value	6 / 3600
Health	400
Strength	60
Resistances (%)	100 Air
	75 Water, 15 Earth, 50 Normal
	60 Fire / Body / Spirit
	60 Mind / Light / Dark
Attacks	Longsword, Throwing Axe
Damage Bonus (%)	+70 Melee
	+20 Ranged
Shield	Tower

Shambler

Level / XP Value	4 / 1600
Health	150
Strength	30
Resistances (%)	30 Normal
	45 Dark, 10 Light
	25 Fire / Earth / Air / Water
	25 Body / Spirit / Mind
Attacks	Mace

Dark Lord, Mage

Level / XP Value	11 / 12100
Health	1000
Strength	90
Resistances (%)	95 Dark, 85 Water
	80 Normal, 50 Light
	75 Fire / Earth / Air / Body / Spirit / Mind
Attacks	Warhammer
	Freezeball (40-70 Dark)
Damage Bonus (%)	+130 Melee
	+30 Ranged
Shield	Tower
Spells	Lightning (2), Mana Shield (2)

NOTE: In the final battle of the game, you face a Dark Lord and Mage with +1 Experience, 200 additional Health points and more magical spells.

Level / XP Value	11 / 12100
Health	800
Strength	65
Resistances (%)	100 Dark
	65 Normal, 85 Water, 60 Light
	75 Fire / Earth / Air / Body / Spirit / Mind
Spells	Firestorm (2)
	Lightning (2), Regeneration (2)
Attacks	Fist (30-60)
Damage Bonus (%)	+80 Melee
	+30 Ranged

Twice-Born
Fighter, Caster

Level / XP Value	5 / 2500
Health	250
Strength	45
Resistances (%)	80 Dark
	55 Normal, 50 Water
	45 Fire / Earth / Air / Body
	45 Spirit / Mind, 25 Light
Spells	Firestorm (1)
Attacks (Caster)	Fist (30-60)
Attacks (Fighter)	Mace. Throwing Axe
Damage Bonus (%)	+30 Melee
	+10 Ranged
Shield (Fighter)	Spiked

FRIENDS & FOES

41

Black Guard Master

Level / XP Value	8 / 6400
Health	750
Strength	80
Resistances (%)	100 Air
	85 Water, 45 Earth
	70 Fire / Body / Spirit / Mind
	70 Light / Dark, 60 Normal
Attacks	Battle Axe
	Exploding Gem (Spirit)
Damage Bonus (%)	+100 Melee
	+20 Ranged
Shield	Tower
Spells	Lightning (2), Heroism (2)

Homunculus

Level / XP Value	8 / 6400
Health	600
Strength	50
Resistances (%)	75 Normal, 50 Spirit
	90 Fire / Water / Body / Mind
	70 Earth / Air / Light / Dark
Attacks	Fist (25-45) (Earth)
Damage Bonus (%)	+40 Melee
	+10 Ranged

Black Guard Hero

Level / XP Value	7 / 4900
Health	600
Strength	70
Resistances (%)	100 Air
	80 Water, 55 Normal, 35 Earth
	65 Fire / Body / Spirit / Mind / Light / Dark
Attacks	Longsword
	Throwing Axe (Dark)
Damage Bonus (%)	+80 Melee
	+20 Ranged
Shield	Tower
Spells	Lightning (1), Regeneration (2)

Homunculus Caster

Level / XP Value	8 / 6400
Health	600
Strength	50
Resistances (%)	75 Normal, 50 Spirit
	90 Fire / Water / Body / Mind
	70 Earth / Air / Light / Dark
Attacks	Fist (25-45) (Earth)
Damage Bonus (%)	+40 Melee
	+10 Ranged

Necros

Dear Celestia,

I have finally completed the inquiry you requested into the nature and origins of Necros. I think you will find that some of your suspicions are confirmed, while some of this information is more surprising. Of course, much remains mysterious.

First of all, I have become quite convinced that Necros, despite popular belief, is not an undead creature of any description. He seems to be a living man, although of an unnatural age (at least 200 years, based on evidence I detail below). He also seems to be invulnerable to most forms of harm. There have been several reported assassination attempts against Necros, both from our side and within the Legion himself. On at least three occasions in the last 50 years, it is reliably recorded that Necros sustained blows that should have proven fatal, only to walk away from the encounters apparently without harm. On one occasion it is reported that he was actually decapitated by one of the commander zombies of his Legion. The report says his headless body reached down, picked up his head and replaced it on his neck, after which he sat very still for several minutes (the attacking retainer having been instantly chopped to bits by more loyal guards). After some time had passed, he abruptly gave his head a vigorous shake and walked out of the room, apparently without harm.

Admittedly this account may be held in some reasonable suspicion, since it comes from a captured officer of the Legion, and may be simply an attempt to demoralize our troops. Much more reliable, however, is the report that some seven years ago, at the second battle of Sho Scarp, a Legion war galleon crashed from a height of about 3000 feet, with such force that even the undead crew was instantly annihilated. Necros, however, was observed to walk out of the burning wreckage several minutes after the crash, and wait without visible concern on the battlefield for several minutes, until he was picked up by another Legion flier.

Nonetheless, he seems to live. It has been reliably reported that he eats, breathes, sleeps and even exercises libidinous impulses of a more-or-less normal nature.

I believe I have traced his origins back at least 150 years. I have uncovered reports from that time of a skilled wizard and necromancer who apparently succeeded in some radical experiments. (His true name is not known, for like many senior practitioners of the necromantic arts, he guarded his true name jealously, lest an enemy wizard use it against him.) These records indicate that this wizard, in seeking to make himself 100 aging, tapped into a far more potent source of power than he had anticipated, and actually made himself unable to die, even by violence or through his own will.

One troubling aspect of these reports which should probably be brought to your attention. There is somewhat ambiguous evidence that in conducting these experiments Necros had a collaborator or patron ... or perhaps I should say patroness, for there is some evidence that it was a female. The fate of this entity is unknown, and raises the possibility that there may be another person with supernatural vitality like Necros' own at large, with unknown motivations or principles. The reports suggest that this person was both powerful and unscrupulous.

These are only the broadest and most important of my conclusions. I am presently compiling a much more detailed report, which I shall communicate at the earliest possible opportunity.

With profound respect,

Arcas, Scholar

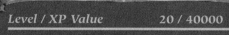

Level / XP Value	20 / 40000
Health	2000
Strength	75
Resistances (%)	100 Dark
	85 Water, 70 Normal, 60 Light
	70 Fire / Earth / Air Body / Spirit / Mind
Spells	Lightning (4)
	Deadly Swarm (3)
	Heroism (4)
Attacks	Fist (25-45) (Air)
Damage Bonus (%)	+100 Melee
	+30 Ranged

ADDENDA: Shortly after completing this dispatch, Arcas the historian was killed in his home in a fire of mysterious origin. No trace of the records he refers to have been found.   – Crusader Archivist.

Crusaders of Might and Magic

Escape from Stronghold

Stronghold was once the mightiest bastion of the Old Guard Crusader knights. Now, it is haunted by the Legion of the Fallen, a hideous army of undead warriors bent on the utter conquest of all living creatures, ruled by the tyrant Necros.

Captured by these undead conquerors, you are cast into the deepest dungeon of Stronghold. You know torture awaits you, presumably followed by a hideous undead existence as a zombie of the Legion. But salvation comes from a most unexpected source. Celestia, leader of the Crusade, contacts you, giving you the power you need to fight your way out of your cell.

With Celestia as your guide, and with only a single spell to defend yourself, you must scavenge what armor, weapons and mystical objects happen to fall into your hands. You face nearly mindless Shambler zombies, and their far more dangerous masters, the Twice–Born, as well as the terrifying Black Guard of Necros.

If you can win free to make contact with the Crusader forces camped outside the walls of Stronghold, then you'll be able to fulfill Celestia's command to report to her at the Citadel.

1

Use your *Fire Storm* spell △ to destroy the Shambler sent to take you to your doom.

2

Collect his money, mace and mana potion.

3

An apparition of Celestia appears in your cell with lots of useful advice.

4

Move through the door into the next room.

5

Another Shambler waits without. Autotarget him R2, then *Fire Storm* him. Collect his treasure, but be careful … the fire beneath the grate he's standing on will injure you.

6

If you've taken damage, the healing potion next to the iron maiden will help.

44

7

You can also jump up ⊗ onto the torture rack for more throwing axes.

8

Mana potions are hidden in the chimney of the fire pit. Jump up into the chimney to get them, but watch out for fire damage from the pit.

9

There are goodies in the next cell. Once you collect the loot on floor level, push the crate under the alcove in the back wall.

10

Jump up on the crate, then up to the alcove to retrieve the healing potions.

11

Go back out to the large chamber, and through the large sliding door.

12

Go left and up the ramp. Get the spiked shield from the dead Crusader.

13

Go back down the ramp and turn left. Be careful to avoid the mine on the floor.

14

Go through the next door. To your left, you will pass your first Save Point. Walk into it.

15

Opposite the Save Point is another cell. Kill the Shambler waiting there and collect all the goodies you find (including the money on the dead Crusader).

HINT At this point in the game, you want to engage the enemy as often as possible ... your first priority is to get your experience level and weapon ranks up.

STRONGHOLD

STRONGHOLD

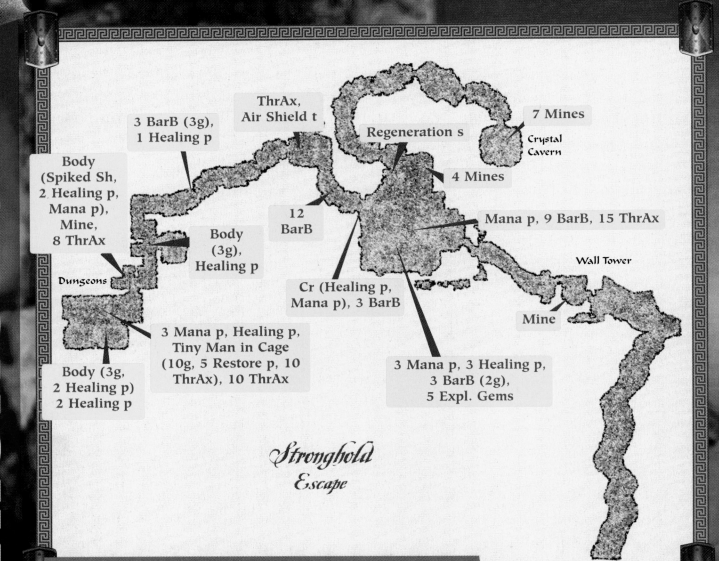

3 BarB (3g),
1 Healing p

ThrAx,
Air Shield t

Regeneration s

7 Mines

Crystal
Cavern

Body
(Spiked Sh,
2 Healing p,
Mana p),
Mine,
8 ThrAx

4 Mines

Body
(3g),
Healing p

12
BarB

Mana p, 9 BarB, 15 ThrAx

Wall Tower

Dungeons

Cr (Healing p,
Mana p), 3 BarB

Mine

3 Mana p, Healing p,
Tiny Man in Cage
(10g, 5 Restore p, 10
ThrAx), 10 ThrAx

3 Mana p, 3 Healing p,
3 BarB (2g),
5 Expl. Gems

Body (3g,
2 Healing p)
2 Healing p

Stronghold

Escape

Encounters

SHAMBLER (20)
Most have 9g.
1 - 10 ThrAx
1 - 21g, Fire Gem, 5 ThrAx
1 - Healing p
2 - Healing p, Mana p
1 - Air Gem, Restore p
1 - Light Gem, 10 ThrAx
1 - Spirit Gem
1 - Spirit Gem, Healing p
1 - ThrAx, Mana p
1 - 2 Mana p, Mace
1 - 5 ThrAx
1 - 5 ThrAx, Healing p

TWICE-BORN (8)
Most have 21g.
1 - 105g, Tower sh,
    5 Restore p
1 - 105g, 5 Mana p, 25 ThrAx
1 - 200g, Fire Armor t, Scale ar
1 - Restore p
1 - Healing p, 2 Mana p
1 - Restore p, 5 ThrAx
1 - Mana p, Air Gem
1 - 2 ThrAx

BLACK GUARD SENTRY
1 - 105g, 2 Expl. gem

Map Key

g = gold
p = potion
t = talisman
s = spell
ar = armor
sh = shield
expl. gem = exploding gem
BarB = barrel bomb
CrB = crate bomb
Bar = barrel
Cr = crate
ThrAx = Throwing Axe

16

Continue down the corridor. Jump up on the boxes for a healing potion.

17

Around the corner two more Shamblers await. If you're quick, you can take them out by blowing up the barrel nearby them, but they'll soon move to attack you.

18

You'll come to a doorway with a Shambler visible on the other side. Kill him with spells or ranged weapons, but don't go through the door …

19

… someone's waiting to jump you just inside the door. Once the first one's dead, run through to the opposite side of the room, turn around and take out the second.

20

In the next room is a talisman between two pillars, but the pillars are trapped with lightning. Move close, wait for the lightning to strike, then dash quickly between the pillars for the talisman. It's an Air Shield Talisman, called Lightning Rune, and it is applied automatically to your shield.

21

In the next room enemies have barricaded themselves behind crates. *Fire Storm* any of the crates in the room to clear out the opposition.

You find your first defensive spell, *Regeneration*, at the door to a room with a statue.

22

The statue is a bust of Necros. It will eventually start throwing lightning at you.

23

You can't fight it, so turn right and run out of the room.

24

In the room with two columns, a *Fire Storm* spell will toast any of the barrels.

25

Beyond the room with the columns is a small courtyard. There are some goodies on the ledge to the right.

STRONGHOLD

26

From the top of the ledge, you can jump forward and grab some Exploding Gems. *If you're interested in a tough battle* with some nice rewards, continue. If you'd like to skip the battle for now, jump to Frame 30, below.

27

Return to the bust of Necros (it won't fire at you any more). Go into First Person mode, and target the statue, then hit it with a continuous series of *Fire Storms* until it's destroyed (it will take a dozen or more hits). This will open the door to the left of the statue.

28

At the very end of a l-o-n-g hallway is a room with two Twice-Born and a Black Guard. Engage them with ranged attacks … you're not tough enough to take them on hand-to-hand yet.

29

If you win this fight, you'll emerge with scale armor, a tower shield and a Flame Talisman (Fire Armor).

30

Return to the room with the pillars. To the right of the entrance is a side-chamber containing a Save Point and an elevator.

31

When you get on the elevator, turn around. This will put you face-to-face with the Shamblers at the top.

32

Once you've cleared the Shamblers, break the case for its potions, then jump on the next elevator. There are two more Shamblers at the top.

33

Go down the hallway until you come to a room with a ramp and a door. The door won't open, so take the ramp. Watch out for the two Shamblers waiting to ambush you from above.

34

At the top of the ramp are a Twice-Born and a Shambler. This Twice-Born isn't as tough as some — you should be able to take him with your mace.

35 Push the crates at the back of the room to get to a trove of throwing axes.

36 Jump up to the small passage at the top of the ramp.

37 The next Save Point is at the top.

38 Head down the passage until you get to the drop-off. There are three platforms going down to the bridge, and you have to hit each one in turn as you jump down.

39 When you hit the bridge, you notice that you're now on the other side of the door you couldn't open earlier. You have to fight a tough Black Guard Sentry.

40 Go through the tower to the second part of the bridge.

41 At the end of the bridge jump up to the box, then up to the wall, and finally up to the second box.

42 Jump across to the mountain path. If you fall, you won't die, but you'll have to fight a Shambler, climb back up to the wall and try again.

43 Make your way carefully up the mountain path, fighting the Shamblers and Twice-Born that guard the way. Be careful … if your enemies can knock you off the path, it means instant death. Better to engage them from a distance. Once you reach the end of the path, your escape from Stronghold is complete.

Citadel

Against all odds, you arrive safely at the Citadel, the floating sky-fortress of the Crusaders. For a short time, you have a respite from deadly adventure, as you roam the halls and chambers of this marvel from another era. From such a fortress, surely the Crusade can mount an effective offensive against Necros and his foul Legion.

Your first task is to seek out Celestia herself, along with her chief lieutenant, Ursan. They invite you to join the ranks of the Crusaders. Although you've always been a lone wolf, you decide you can be more effective in your personal vendetta against Necros if you ally with the Crusade. Once you're enlisted, you receive your first mission, to act as Celestia's emissary to the underground Dwarven nation of Corantha. Joining the Crusade also entitles you to report to Korinda, the quartermaster of Citadel, who'll issue you improved arms and armor.

There are other secrets to be found in the halls of Citadel, but eventually you will have to leave its comforts, and continue the quest that is your destiny.

Upon your escape from Stronghold, you find yourself on a sandy beach being guarded by Crusaders. One of the guards instructs you to catch the ferry to the Citadel.

Continue down the beach until you get to a heavy, guarded door.

To the right of the door and up a short path is a Save Point.

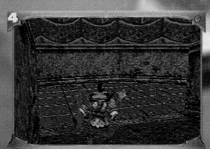

Go through the stone doors and ride the lift up.

You meet Aerrin, the air-ship pilot who will carry you to the Citadel.

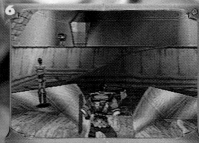

Disembark at the air-dock.

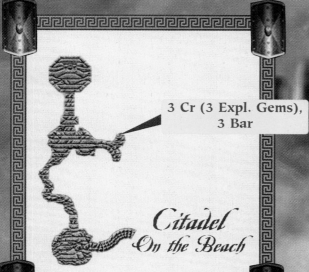

3 Cr (3 Expl. Gems),
3 Bar

Citadel
On the Beach

Encounters

HIGH GUARD CRUSADER (1)
1 - 50g, Dark Gem

OLD GUARD CRUSADER (5)
4 - 9g, Spirit Gem,
　2 Expl. gems
1 - 9g, Spirit Gem,
　Restore p

CITADEL

Encounters

DARK MAGE (1)
1 - 489g, Restore p,
　Dark Gem

GLACIER FERRY PILOT (1)
1 - 9g, Spirit Gem, 2 ThrAx

OLD GUARD - JOHNATHAN
1 - 9g, Spirit Gem, 2 ThrAx

OLD GUARD - PETROS
1 - 9g, Spirit Gem, 2 ThrAx

HIGH GUARD (8)
8 - 9g, Dark Gem

MERCHANT (1)
1 - 9g

MOURNING CRUSADER (1)
1 - 9g, Spirit Gem, 2 ThrAx

OLD GUARD CRUSADER (14)
14 - 9g, Spirit Gem,
　2 ThrAx

TWICE-BORN (2)
2 - 105g, 2 ThrAx

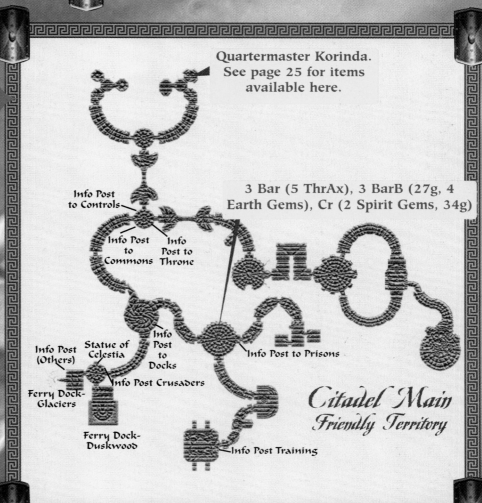

Quartermaster Korinda.
See page 25 for items
available here.

3 Bar (5 ThrAx), 3 BarB (27g, 4
Earth Gems), Cr (2 Spirit Gems, 34g)

Info Post
to Controls

Info Post　Info
to　　　Post to
Commons　Throne

Info Post to Prisons

Info Post
(Others)　Statue of　Info
　　　Celestia　Post
　　　　　　to
　　　　　　Docks

Ferry Dock-　　Info Post Crusaders
Glaciers

Ferry Dock-
Duskwood

Info Post Training

Citadel Main
Friendly Territory

From the ferry, go straight ahead into the guard room, then turn right and head up the sloping passage.

You come to a large room with a ramp up, and an exit to the right. There's a Save Point in an alcove under the ramp. Take the ramp up.

After a long hall, you come to a room with two exits, one to the left and one ahead.

HINT Be careful not to accidentally attack any of the guards in the Citadel. They *will* defend themselves.

The guard at the exit opposite where you entered will speak to you. His name is Nikolai, and he wants you to tell his brother, Johnathan, to pay up on a gambling debt. Johnathan works in the prison.

Go through the door Nikolai was guarding and cross the bridge. You pass a small glowing room on your right, with a Save Point in it.

You come to a small outdoor area. The only exit has a red carpet. Follow the carpet.

This takes you to Celestia's throne room, where you can talk to Celestia and Ursan for your mission. Technically, this ends your second quest, but there's more to do in Citadel.

In the alcoves around the room is a wealth of information about the various regions of the land.

Go back the way you came, over the bridge. When you get back to Nikolai's post, take a right.

16

You come to a room with two exits, one of which is covered by a blue force screen. If you try to cross the threshold, a guard will tell you that access to the Light Lance is forbidden. Leave via the other exit.

17

You come to another blue force screen, this one guarding the Bridge, the control center for the Citadel.

18

Across from the Bridge is the Quartermaster, Korinda. She issues you the equipment Celestia promised, and allows you to browse for other useful items.

HINT *You probably won't be able to afford armor, weapons or talismans, but you can stock up on ranged weapons and potions.*

19

Retrace your steps all the way back to the big room with the ramp. If you hit the chandelier which hangs over this room with a *Fire Storm* spell, it will spill out two healing potions and three exploding gems. At the bottom of the ramp take the door to the left.

20

You come to an open area. Search the crates and barrels for goodies, then exit through the door opposite the one you came in by.

21

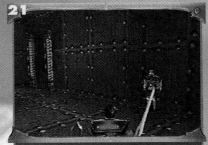

Up the hallway is the prison, and Brother Johnathan. Shake him down for his brother's money.

22

Also in the prison is a captive Dark Mage who'll recognize you.

23

Go back to the open courtyard and take the exit to your left. Go down the hall to the barracks, where a guard mentions that there's a training room up the next hall.

24

Between the barracks and the training room, you find a Save Point.

CITADEL

CITADEL

25 The training room turns out to be a series of floating platforms you have to jump to. If you fall, you fall right out of Citadel, all the way to the ground, and that's a long way down …

26 … however, if you make it to the top platform, you get the *Snap Freeze* spell.

27 Now you need to return to Nikolai and give him his money. He gives you a fire gem in return, and tells you to talk to his other brother, Petros, who guards the Quartermaster.

28 Petros will give you his battle axe, in appreciation for helping his brother.

29 Return to Nikolai. He won't talk to you; you're just giving Petros some space.

30 Now return to Petros. He asks you to carry a talisman to his Lieutenant, who's guarding the throne room.

31 In the throne room, the Lieutenant is guarding the left force screen. He generously allows you to keep Ohkam's Talisman (it's Mind Armor). He also gives you a message to deliver to one of his men, the next time you visit the beach.

32 Now that you've cleaned out Citadel, don't forget to save on your way out.

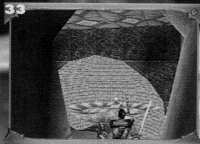

33 At the dock, you find Aerrin waiting to take you on your next mission.

Journey to Corantha

To begin your mission to the Dwarves, you are taken to the outskirts of Duskwood, the great forest. The road to Corantha is not far … so long as you don't take a wrong turning. The Dashers, the mysterious inhabitants of Duskwood, have no love for strangers, and will seek your life with every step.

When you do arrive at the underground kingdom of Corantha, you find that all is not well. King Aiden is dead, and the land is torn by rebellion. You must fight your way through rebel traps and ambushes. Along the way, you may be able to rescue Castor, the master-smith, who will show his appreciation.

At last you make your way to the council chamber, where the current rulers of Corantha strive to return order to their people. They are Dain and Tor, the sons of King Aiden, and the warleader General Martel.

You are firmly told that the Crusade can expect no aid from the Dwarves until the rebellion is quashed. Impetuously, you volunteer to fight your way deep into rebel territory, and ferret out the identity of the mysterious traitor who commands the rebels.

Aerrin deposits you atop a pile of rocks in Duskwood.

You come to a clearing with three exits (the one to the right is covered by webs). Take the one straight ahead.

You come to a fork in the road. The right fork is where you're ultimately heading, but for now take the left.

Defeat the first Dasher you meet, and you'll be rewarded with the powerful Body Weapon talisman. You can continue and fight more Dashers for experience if you want, but eventually you'll have to go back to the fork in the road and head right.

Immediately beyond the fork to the right is a Save Point.

TO CORANTHA

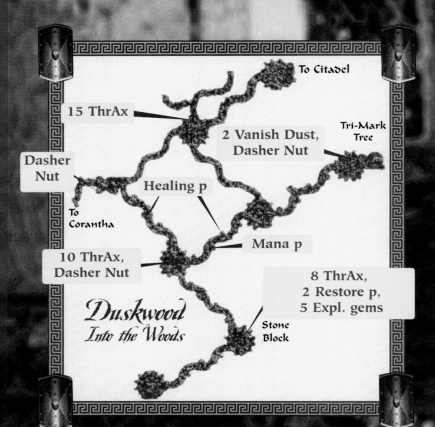

Map labels:
- To Citadel
- 15 ThrAx
- 2 Vanish Dust, Dasher Nut
- Tri-Mark Tree
- Dasher Nut
- Healing p
- To Corantha
- Mana p
- 10 ThrAx, Dasher Nut
- 8 ThrAx, 2 Restore p, 5 Expl. gems
- *Duskwood* Into the Woods
- Stone Block

Encounters

DASHER BRUTE (5)
Most have 69g.
1 - 28g, Nut, Restore p
1 - 2 Healing p
2 - Earth Gem, Healing p
1 - Nut, Healing p

DASHER SCOUT (5)
1 - 31g, Mana p, Nut
2 - 41g, 2 ThrAx, Vanish Dust
1 - 59g, 3 Spirit Gem, 3 Restore p
1 - Body Weapon t, Nut, Vanish Dust

OGRE (6)
1 - 35g, Mana p
1 - 41g, 2 ThrAx, Mana p
1 - 41g, Restore p
1 - 50g, Mana p
1 - 56g
1 - 5g, Healing p

6

Head into the cave to enter Corantha.

7

First, head right along the cliff face.

8

You come to a pair of barrels. Destroy them both, then look up (in First Person Mode) for a third barrel way up high on the cliff. Destroy it with a throwing axe for goodies.

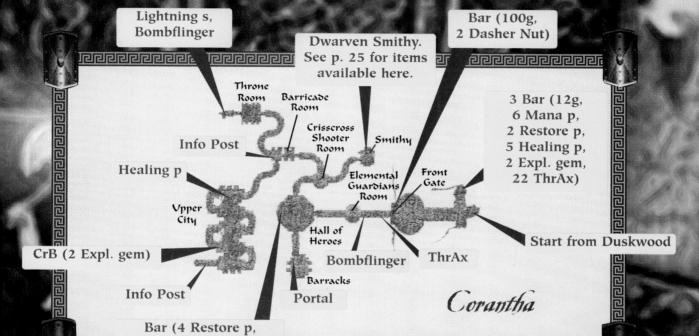

Lightning s, Bombflinger

Dwarven Smithy. See p. 25 for items available here.

Bar (100g, 2 Dasher Nut)

Throne Room

Barricade Room

Crisscross Shooter Room

Smithy

3 Bar (12g, 6 Mana p, 2 Restore p, 5 Healing p, 2 Expl. gem, 22 ThrAx)

Info Post

Healing p

Elemental Guardians Room

Front Gate

Upper City

Hall of Heroes

Start from Duskwood

CrB (2 Expl. gem)

Bombflinger

ThrAx

Info Post

Barracks

Portal

Corantha

Bar (4 Restore p, 5 Fire gem, 5 Air gem)

Encounters

STONEHEART REGULAR (9)
All have 9g.
7 - 3 ThrAx

IRONPICK REBEL (15)
All have 21g.
1 - Healing p
1 - Mana p
1 - Fire Shield t

IRONPICK MAGE (2)
2 - 69g, Body Gem,
  2 Restore p

IRONPICK ZEALOT (6)
6 - 41g, Expl. gem

STONE ELEMENTAL (2)
2 - Earth Gem

There is a Save Point near the barrels.

TO CORANTHA

TO CORANTHA

Now you can cross the bridge.

As you approach the gates, rebels emerge and kill the guards (you can't save them). When they find out you're from Celestia, the rebels will attack you.

Dispatch the rebels, then enter through the large stone doors.

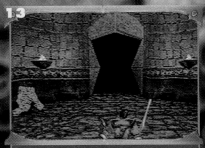

You come to a room guarded by two inert Earth Elementals. As you pass, they animate and attack you. This will be a tough fight.

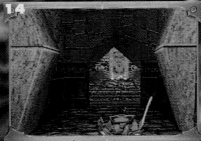

You come to the Hall of Heroes. Mages are waiting inside to ambush you with fireballs, so quickly run in and go through the door to the left.

Engage the two rebels in the corridor. Watch out! The mages behind you might jump down and ambush you from behind.

Talk to the guard behind the force screen. He'll give you directions to the Throne Room.

Return to the Hall of Heroes and take care of any mages that remain.

Climb up to the ledges the mages were on (jump up to the red blocks, then climb the wall to the ledge), and destroy the barrels for some goodies.

19

Leave the Hall of Heroes by the right exit. You come to a large room guarded by automatic explosive missile shooters. Run through the opposite exit.

20

At the end of the hallway is Castor, the Dwarven Smithy, under attack by rebels. If you help him out, he'll give you Ice Claw (Water Weapon talisman), and directions to the Throne Room.

21

Castor also operates a merchant shop where you can stock up on necessities.

22
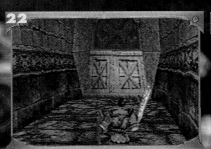
Go back to the room with the explosive missiles, and take a right through the double doors.

23

You come to a guard under attack by a pair of rebels. Help him out (but be careful not to attack the guard by mistake, or he'll defend himself … vigorously).

24

Follow the red carpet to the Throne Room, where Dain will give you your next quest.

25

Leave the Throne Room the way you came. At the first right, you find a Save Point.

TO CORANTHA

The Ironpick Rebellion

You fight your way down into the bowels of the Dwarven kingdom. When you make a dizzying leap over a bottomless chasm, from one fragment of a demolished bridge to another, you know that there is no turning back.

Down here the Ironpicks are firmly in control. Nearly everybody you meet is your enemy. You begin your one-man invasion with sabotage: blowing up an Ironpick armory. Along the way you rescue Pollux the smith, brother to your friend Castor. Pollux promises you a suitable reward when you next visit the smithy he shares with his brother.

At last your search pays off. From the perilous safety of a ventilation duct, you overhear a conference between the leader of the rebellion and Necros himself! You discover that the chief rebel is none other than Prince Tor.

Your only remaining task is to escape alive to bring this news to the Stonehearts. With perseverance, however, you can uncover the route back across the broken bridge and up to the council chamber again.

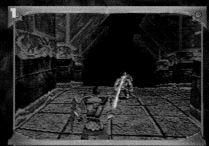

The first leg of your journey is a run down a long hall where Stoneheart Regulars are fighting Ironpick Rebels and Zealots.

This barricade hides goodies.

You finally reach the entrance to the menacing Coranthan mines.

There's a Save Point to your right as you enter.

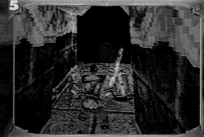

A wounded dwarf tells you that the bridge has been destroyed by Ironpick Rebels.

All is not lost. From the edge of the chasm …

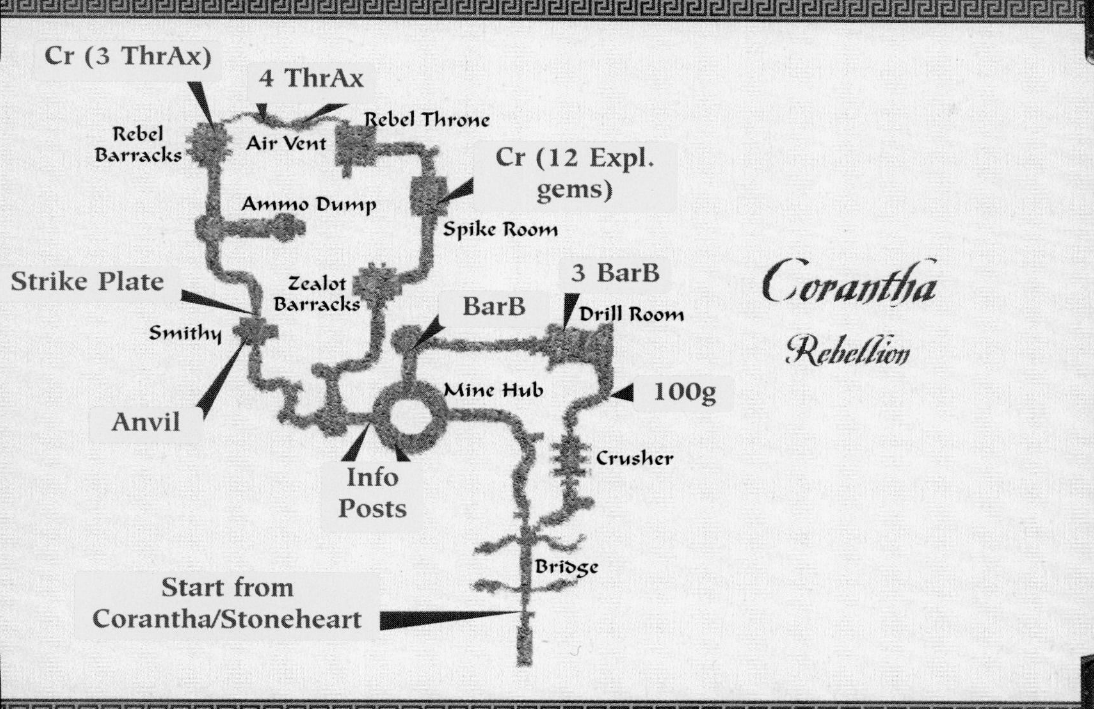

Cr (3 ThrAx)

4 ThrAx

Rebel Throne

Rebel Barracks

Air Vent

Cr (12 Expl. gems)

Ammo Dump

Spike Room

Strike Plate

Zealot Barracks

3 BarB

Corantha

Rebellion

Smithy

BarB

Drill Room

Mine Hub

100g

Anvil

Crusher

Info Posts

Bridge

Start from Corantha/Stoneheart

REBELLION

Encounters

STONEHEART REGULAR (1)
1 - 9g, 3 ThrAx

MERCHANT POLLUX (1)
1 - 9g, 5 Expl. gem

IRONPICK REBEL (7)
Most have 21g.
5 - 2 Expl. gem, Mana p
1 - 41g, 2 Expl. gem

IRONPICK ZEALOT (23)
5 - 2 Expl. gem
6 - 41g, Expl. gem
12 - 41g, 2 Expl. gem

… you can leap down to a support pillar. You will take damage from this leap, so be prepared to heal yourself.

From there you can jump to the entrance to a lower tunnel (taking a bit more damage).

REBELLION

Just inside this tunnel is another Save Point.

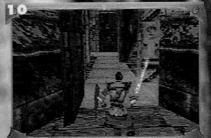

You have to pass through a room where crushers can instantly kill you. Run up to the crushers when they're closed, then dash through as soon as they're open to make it past them.

Move these oar carts around to find 100 gold, then use them to leap the barricade.

You arrive at a large room just as a Coranthan drill breaks through the wall …

… allowing you to take the newly created passageway.

You discover a large, circular room with elevators going up and down.

For now, take the elevator going up.

The only passage out from this room leads to three Ironpick Dwarves waiting to ambush you.

They're guarding Pollux, the Dwarven smith.

18

His cell is opened with a switch on the wall in the next hallway.

19

As you enter the next room, the gate will snap shut behind you. That's OK, though ...

20

... because you've found the Ironpick Rebel ammo dump. One well-placed *Fire Storm* will take care of it. Technically, this completes your quest, except for the minor detail of getting back out alive!

21

Return to the room with the gates, and blow the explosive barrels with a *Fire Storm* to open the way out.

22

You enter a two-level room with one Ironpick Rebel on the floor and two above. Beware overhead snipers!

23

Climb up the central pillars to the upper deck, and crawl into the small ventilation shaft.

24

The shaft contains turning blades. Time your passage carefully, and don't stop in the blades' shadow.

25

You find an opening, where you witness an incriminating conference between Necros and Prince Tor. Unfortunately, they'll get away before you can take action.

26

To avoid too much falling damage, jump down to one of the braziers below, then jump off quickly, before it can burn you.

REBELLION

27

You can't open the secret door by which the villains escaped, so take the exit and continue on.

28

The room beyond the broken gate is filled with hostile Ironpick Zealots.

29

The center column in the room can be climbed to escape.

30

From the upper platform, jump over the grate.

31

In the next two-level room, the exit is on the floor level.

32

There's a Save Point on the right wall.

33

At the next intersection, turn left. You're back at the elevator hub. This time go down to the bottom level.

34

You're now on the other side of the broken bridge. Jump across as you did before.

35

The wall on the opposite cliff face has footholds, allowing you to climb up to where you started.

36

Return to the Throne Room and talk to Dain and Martel. They'll give you your next quest.

37

Don't forget to stop at the Smithy to collect your reward from Castor and Pollux.

38

Leave Corantha and return to Duskwood. This is a great time to save your game!

Scepter of Regency

Returning to the council chamber, you discover that the treacherous Prince Tor has already fled for his cowardly life. Crown Prince Dain Stoneheart, the rightful heir, is now ready to take the throne and swear an alliance with the Crusade, but one vital detail remains. The Dwarven Scepter of Regency has been stolen by the Thunder Clan Ogres of Duskwood. Until the scepter is recovered, there can be no coronation ... and no alliance. Once again, you are forced to volunteer.

Visiting the Dwarven brothers in their smithy, you discover that Castor and Pollux, despite their rough manner, are properly grateful for your help.

In Duskwood, you invade the territory of the Ogre Clansman. It soon becomes obvious that you will not be able to retrieve the scepter without help. When you free a captive Dasher named Djad, he promises to help you gain the trust of his suspicious folk. He tells you to meet him at the sacred Tri-Mark tree. But when you arrive, you find your new friend is mortally wounded. You must continue alone.

You fight your way through the brutal gauntlet of traps and ambushes that guard the Dasher village. When you at last reach the heart of Dasher territory, you are told that you've earned the right to meet with Tamris, the Dasher Chieftain.

Tamris tells you that if you can pass a two-part test, you may join the tribe and count on the help of the Dashers. First, you must defeat the mystical Spirit of the Wood, then you must test your might against Tamris himself.

With the Dashers' help, you are at last ready to invade the stronghold of the Thunder Clan, kill their chief and take the Scepter of Regency.

1. As you leave Corantha (and don't forget to save at the entrance), take a right at the first fork.

2. When you come to an Ogre campfire, deal with the Ogres, then go straight on.

HINT

Ogres are Body creatures, so your Body Talisman won't do them much harm. You'll do far better if you place another talisman on the weapon you use.

3

As you fight your way past the Ogre Clansmen, you eventually encounter a hole in the ground.

4

In the hole is an underground Save Point. You'll find several of these in the forest. You can exit the hole by climbing up the wall.

5

You come to a ring of giant mushrooms surrounding a rock. Jump up to the rock to get the *Mana Shield* spell.

6

Leave the clearing via the path to the right of the marked stone.

7

You come to a cave. Kill the Ogre Clansmen guarding it, and the entrance will open. The cave is filled with cages holding captive Dashers. The guard is a powerful Ogre Shaman who can cast spells. (Use your new *Mana Shield* spell for protection.)

8

Kill him and the cages will open. One of the captives, Djad, will speak to you. He'll promise to help you find the scepter, but only after he warns his people about the Ogres.

9

Return to the Ogre campfire, and this time take the right-hand path, through the tree arch.

10

At the next clearing, continue straight — through another tree arch.

11

There's another underground Save Point along this path.

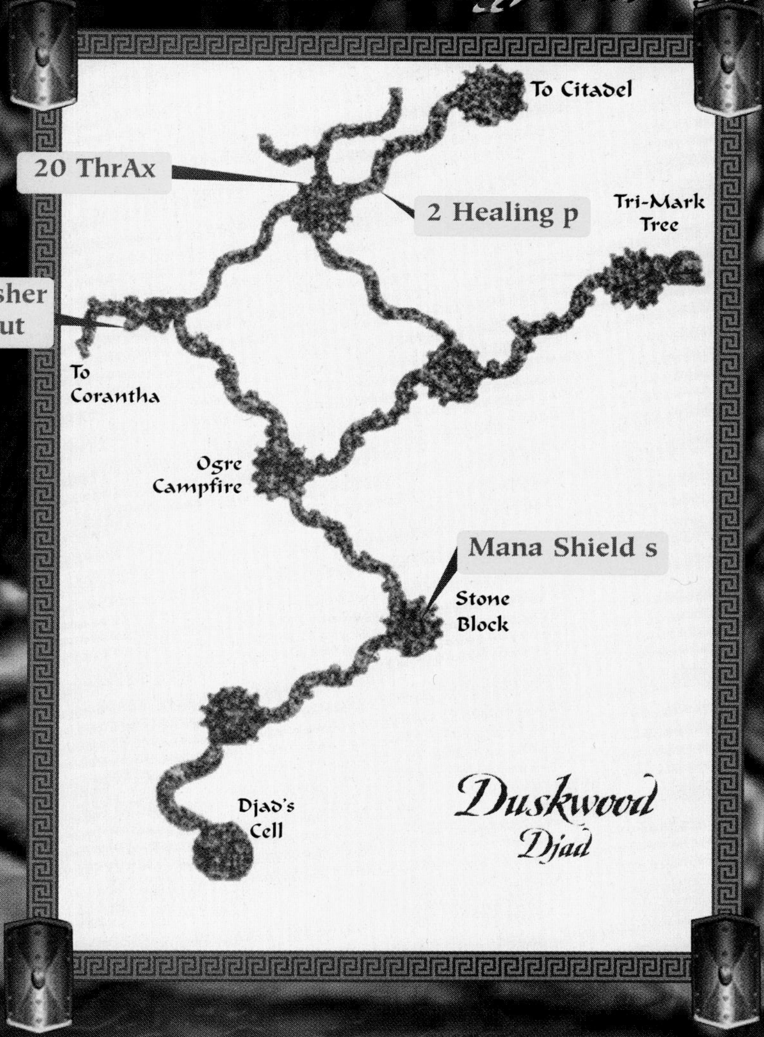

Map — Duskwood / Djad

- To Citadel
- 20 ThrAx
- 2 Healing p
- Tri-Mark Tree
- Dasher Nut
- To Corantha
- Ogre Campfire
- Mana Shield s
- Stone Block
- Djad's Cell

Duskwood
Djad

Encounters

OGRE (16)
Most have 41g.
1 - 32g, Mana p
1 - 32g, Nut
1 - 34g, Restore p
2 - 2 Healing p
7 - 2 ThrAx
1 - 2 ThrAx, Mana p
2 - Restore p
1 - 43g, Mana p, 3 Expl. gem

OGRE SHAMAN (6)
5 - 105g, 2 Restore p
1 - 54g, 2 Restore p,
   Healing p

OLD GUARD CRUSADER (1)
1 - 9g, Spirit Gem, 2 ThrAx

DASHER SCOUT (2)
1 - 105g, Spirit Gem,
   2 Mana p
1 - 2 Mana p

SCEPTER

Soon you arrive at the Tri-Mark tree, where Djad waits. Sadly, he's too heavily wounded to continue. His last request is for you to continue to his village.

TIP

Djad leaves you the Deadly Swarm spell to help you on your way.

Jump up and enter the Tri-Mark tree.

SCEPTER

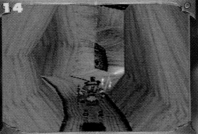

14

There's a Save Point off to your right.

15

You are attacked by Dashers as soon as you leave the Tri-Mark tree.

16

You come to a suspended bridge that you have to jump across. If you fall, you'll have to fight the creatures at the bottom, climb up the vines to your starting point, and try again.

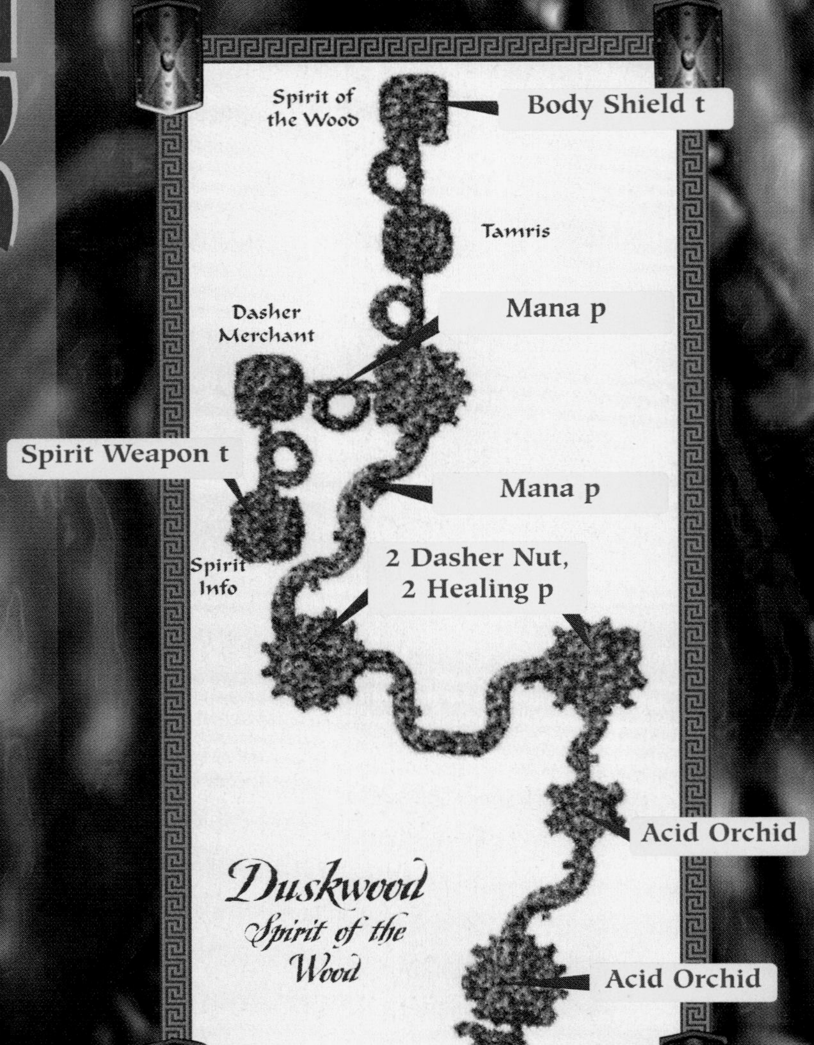

Map labels:

Spirit of the Wood — Body Shield t

Tamris

Mana p

Dasher Merchant

Spirit Weapon t

Mana p

Spirit Info

2 Dasher Nut, 2 Healing p

Acid Orchid

Duskwood
Spirit of the Wood

Acid Orchid

Encounters

DASHER BRUTE (11)
All have Earth Gem, Healing p.
10 - 69g
1 - Heroism s

DASHER MERCHANT — T'POK (1)
1 - 69g, Earth Gem, Healing p

DASHER SCOUT (8)
1 - 105g, Spirit Gem, Fire Gem
3 - 105g, Spirit Gem, 2 Mana p
1 - 2 Mana p
3 - 41g, 2 ThrAx, Vanish Dust

SCEPTER

17 The next open area is a death-trap filled with attacking plants. Don't try to fight your way through, just run as quickly as possible, taking the exit to your left.

18 You come to a steep drop in the path. When you start down, you'll slide all the way to the bottom. From this point, there's no returning to the last Save Point!

19 You come to another garden of death. This time the exit is to the right, near the enormous mushroom.

20 You come to what looks like another underground Save Point. In fact, it's an ambush, but you'll want to go there anyway (if you're strong enough). One of the waiting Dashers carries the *Heroism* spell.

21 At last you come to the Dasher village. You've earned the right to be heard, and the guards won't attack unprovoked.

22 Enter the treetrunk straight ahead of you.

HINT *Dashers are Spirit creatures and are especially vulnerable to your Body talisman, so place that on your weapon.*

23 You arrive in the throne room of Tamris, the Dasher Chieftain.

24 Tamris tells you that you must join his tribe by passing the Test of Spirit. The entrance is directly behind his throne.

25 To pass the test you must touch the spirit of the Heart of Wood.

SCEPTER

26

You must jump up to where it hovers, while it casts *Deadly Swarm* at you.

27

If you succeed, you are rewarded by the Blood Rune (the Body Shield talisman).

28

When you return to the throne room, Tamris tells you that you must fight him for leadership of the tribe if you want Dasher help. If you can survive a few rounds of his attacks and *Snap Freeze* spells, he'll yield. The Dashers are now at your disposal.

29

Leave Tamris' tree and enter the tree "next door." You'll come to the shop of the merchant T'Pok.

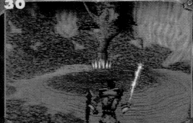

30

Beyond T'Pok's shop is a glade where the Spirit of the Wood will bestow the Soul Bastion (Spirit Weapon) talisman upon you.

31

On the way back to the Dasher village from T'Pok's, you might notice this potion hidden in the ceiling.

32

As a member of the Dasher tribe, you can use the Spirit Gem to teleport you past the gauntlet.

HINT *Equip Soul Bastion on your weapon. It is the best Talisman against the Ogre Clansmen.*

33

When you come to a clearing, go straight through.

34

Take the left path at the campfire area.

35

There's an underground Save Point along this route.

36

Return to the mushroom clearing again.

37

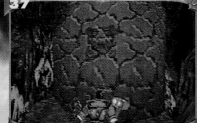

The large stone now looks cracked and fragile.

38

Clear your path by hitting it with a blunt weapon.

39

Continue across a bridge …

40

… then jump across a hanging bridge.

41

You come to the entrance to the Ogre lair.

42

Fortunately, there's a Save Point just inside.

43

Kill all the Ogres in the first room, and the exit opens.

44

You come to a fork in the path. Go left.

SCEPTER

45 At the next open area you again have to slay all the Ogres to open the exit.

46 Pass through the door to the lair of the Ogre Clan Leader.

47 Needless to say the chief is a tough fight, with lots of spells. Defeat him, and you get two (!) talismans — Rune of the Deeps (Water Shield) and the Sinew Talisman (Body Armor).

48 At the chief's death, the door to the Scepter of Regency will also open. Grab it.

49 Return the way you came. Where the caves fork, go left.

50 Hit the switch (you'll have to jump) to open the way out.

51 Go through one clearing.

52 You arrive back at the giant mushroom yet again.

53 Take the left exit to the campfire and continue straight through. At the next intersection you meet your last Ogre Clansman. Defeat him and go left.

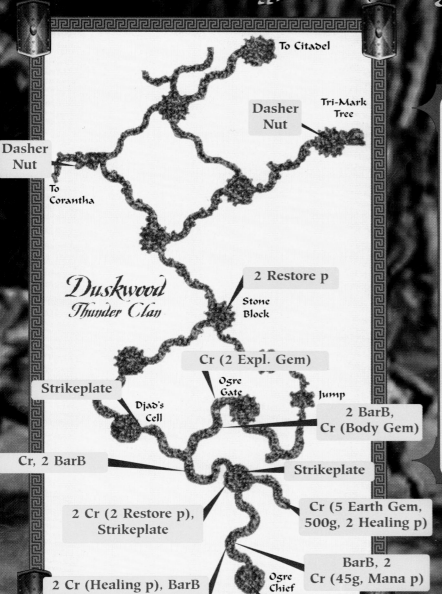

To Citadel

Dasher Nut

Tri-Mark Tree

Dasher Nut

To Corantha

Dasher Nut

Duskwood
Thunder Clan

2 Restore p

Stone Block

Cr (2 Expl. Gem)

Ogre Gate

Jump

Strikeplate

Djad's Cell

2 BarB, Cr (Body Gem)

Cr, 2 BarB

Strikeplate

2 Cr (2 Restore p), Strikeplate

Cr (5 Earth Gem, 500g, 2 Healing p)

BarB, 2 Cr (45g, Mana p)

2 Cr (Healing p), BarB

Ogre Chief

Scepter of Regency

Encounters

OGRE (11)

Most have 41g.
7 - 2 ThrAx
1 - 2 ThrAx, Mana p
2 - Restore p
1 - 43g, Mana p, 3 Expl. gem

OGRE LEADER (1)

1 - 150g, Body Armor t,
   Water Shield t

OGRE SHAMAN (6)

5 - 105g, 2 Restore p
1 - 54g, 2 Restore p, Healing p

OLD GUARD CRUSADER (1)

1 - 9g, Spirit Gem, 2 ThrAx

DASHER SCOUT (2)

1 - 105g, Spirit Gem, 2 Mana p
1 - 2 Mana p

54

At last you return to the entrance to Corantha.

Stoneheart Rescue

RESCUE

When you return the scepter to Corantha, you find that the situation has deteriorated in your absence. The kingdom has been overrun by Stone and Lava Elementals. Even worse, in the council chamber you find only General Martel, who gives you the horrifying news that the body of King Aiden has been stolen, and Prince Dain has been kidnapped. You are the only one with a prayer of recovering them.

Once again you descend into deep Corantha, fighting elemental invaders and remnants of the Ironpick rebels. Making your way into a newly opened section of the kingdom, you are terrified, but not surprised, to find that the Twice-Born servants of Necros are behind the elemental attack.

When you discover the prison that holds Crown Prince Dain, the remains of Aiden, and the traitor Tor (now you know how Necros treats servants who fail him), you must first defeat the powerful Elemental Lord that guards them. When the elemental falls, the Stonehearts are released but, hideously, the corpse of King Aiden revives as an undead monster. Tor runs immediately, while Dain cannot bear to face his own father in combat. You are left alone against the revenant, in what is certainly the most deadly fight you have ever experienced.

Surely now Dain must be ready to take the throne and swear a pact, but there's no time for thanks or rest. To your surprise and disgust, Celestia teleports you from the council chamber directly to Stronghold, where a completely new mission awaits you.

When you enter Corantha, you're attacked by Elementals. You may also notice a strange lack of Dwarves.

As you pass through the Hall of Heroes, you may also notice that King Aiden's body is gone.

Castor and Pollux are fine though. Drop in and they'll give you a Flame (Fire Armor) Talisman.

HINT *You don't have a talisman that directly opposes Earth yet, so you don't get a bonus against ordinary Stone Elementals. However, some Elementals use Fire Storm, and are aligned with Fire. Your Water Talisman is a big help against these Lava Elementals.*

4

In the Throne Room, only General Martel is left. He explains that Dain went in search of his father's body and his fugitive traitor brother.

5

Fight your way down to the bridge. It's still out — you'll have to jump.

6

The crushers are turned off, but the room is guarded by a fire-wielding Elemental.

HINT *If you want more experience, you can go around again in the same circuit you took the last time you were in Corantha. However, you don't have to follow the old route past this point. If you do follow the old route, you'll find a Flame Talisman (Fire Armor) in the Ammo Depot, if you failed to pick one up from Castor and Pollux for any reason.*

7

The drill has been pushed a bit further into the rock. It's opened up a new passage. Take it.

8

Don't neglect the Save Point on your right.

9

When you get to the digger, turn left.

10

Run quickly through this chamber to minimize fire damage. Falling into the lava pits means instant death.

11

Next is a room with Stone Elementals on one side of a chasm and a Lava Elemental on the other. Jump across. The Lava Elemental will drop the Flamefang (Fire Weapon) talisman when killed.

12

Continue on. There's a Save Point on your right.

RESCUE

75

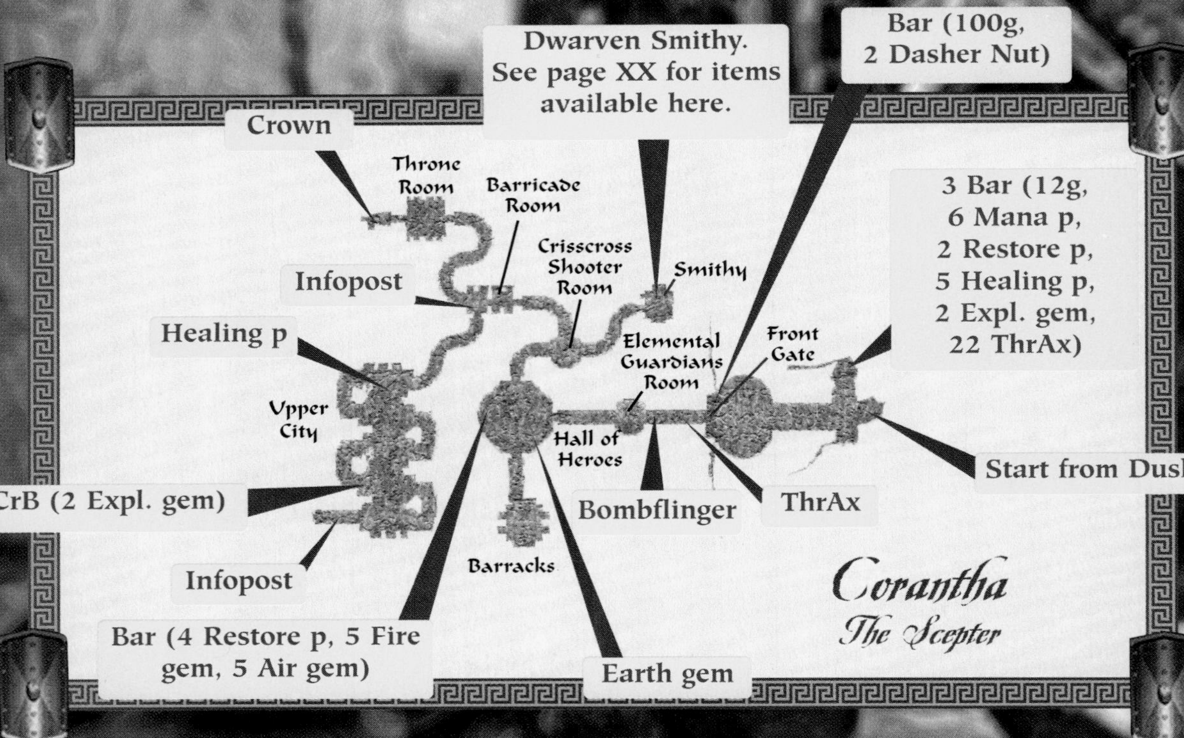

RESCUE

Crown

Throne Room

Barricade Room

Dwarven Smithy. See page XX for items available here.

Bar (100g, 2 Dasher Nut)

Crisscross Shooter Room

Smithy

3 Bar (12g, 6 Mana p, 2 Restore p, 5 Healing p, 2 Expl. gem, 22 ThrAx)

Infopost

Healing p

Elemental Guardians Room

Front Gate

Upper City

Hall of Heroes

CrB (2 Expl. gem)

ThrAx

Infopost

Bombflinger

Start from Duskwood

Barracks

Corantha
The Scepter

Bar (4 Restore p, 5 Fire gem, 5 Air gem)

Earth gem

Encounters

STONEHEART REGULAR (9)
All have 9g, 3 ThrAx.
1 - 2 Healing p

IRONPICK REBEL (13)
All have 21g.
5 - Healing p

IRONPICK ZEALOT (11)
11 - 41g, Expl. gem

STONE ELEMENTAL (5)
All have Earth Gem.
1 - 2 Restore p

LAVA ELEMENTAL (1)
1 - Fire Gem, 2 Mana p

13

You pass through a room with more Elementals and a river of lava.

14

The next room contains a Lava Elemental and several Twice-Born. Are you surprised to find out that the Legion is involved?

RESCUE

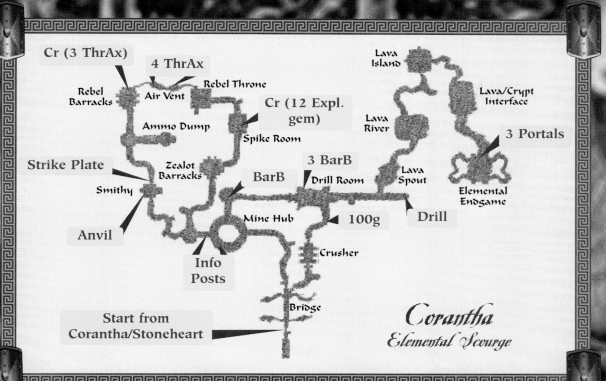

Cr (3 ThrAx)

4 ThrAx

Rebel Throne

Cr (12 Expl. gem)

Rebel Barracks

Air Vent

Ammo Dump

Spike Room

Lava Island

Lava/Crypt Interface

Lava River

3 Portals

Strike Plate

Zealot Barracks

3 BarB

Lava Spout

Smithy

BarB

Drill Room

Elemental Endgame

Anvil

Mine Hub

100g

Drill

Info Posts

Crusher

Start from Corantha/Stoneheart

Bridge

Corantha
Elemental Scourge

The Lava Elemental will drop the Glacial Talisman (Water Armor) when killed. When everything is dead, the golden doors will open.

15

16

The next room is crawling with Stone Elementals, which leaves you with no choice but to ...

Encounters

STONEHEART REGULAR (1)
1 - 9g, 3 ThrAx

IRONPICK REBEL (19)
Most have 21g.
8 - 2 ThrAx, Mana p
6 - 69g, Body Gem, Restore p

IRONPICK ZEALOT (7)
7 - 41g, Expl. gem

STONE ELEMENTAL (11)
7 - Earth Gem
4 - 2 Restore p

STONE ELEMENTAL LORD (4)
1 - 1500g, 6 Restore p
1 - Fire Gem, 2 Mana p
1 - Fire Gem, Fire Weapon t
1 - Water Armor t, 2 Mana p

TWICE-BORN (5)
5 - Dark Gem, 10 ThrAx

RESCUE

17 ... kill them all, and the doors in the corners will open. It doesn't matter which one you go down.

18 At the bottom you'll find Dain, Tor and the body of Aiden all imprisoned in giant crystals.

HINT

You're about to begin what may be the toughest fight in the game. Go back and save, make sure you're fully healed, and cast Regeneration or Heroism.

19 When you touch the crystals, a blue force screen will cover the exits, and an Elemental Lord will appear.

20 When the Elemental Lord is dead, the crystals shatter. The corpse of King Aiden rises as a revenant. Tor bugs out, and Dain can't deal with fighting his father's ghost, so you have to take care of business.

TIP

Your best weapon against the Elemental Lord is a high-rank Lightning spell.

21 When Aiden's finally, really, most sincerely dead, a red screen will appear in the room. Step through it ...

HINT

Aiden is a nightmare (see p. 33). Cast Regeneration — it will save your life. Don't stand and trade blows with Aiden; try to keep him off-balance with a barrage of high-power spells. Be ready to Heal every time you're hit. If necessary, jump into one of the alcoves at the back of the room to heal up ... he has trouble hitting you there.

22

… and it will take you directly to the Throne Room, where Dain will finally pledge an alliance with Celestia.

23

As you leave the Throne Room, Celestia appears and teleports you directly back to the Citadel, where you'll receive a new mission.

24

On your way out, check in with the Quartermaster, and upgrade all armor, spells and talismans you can afford.

25

Aerrin is out on another mission, so an Old Guard Crusader pilot will take you to your next quest.

The Glaciers

Next, the Old Guard Crusader and his trusty ferry transport you to the frozen land of the Glaciers. Apparently you're supposed to retrieve another toy for Celestia's collection — the Star of Erathia. It was once intended as a gift for the Lord Protectors of Stronghold. However, the magical Star was lost after the *Skyseeker* airship crashed in one of the frequent storms over this frigid wasteland.

No welcoming committee awaits. Almost immediately, you get a rude introduction to more elemental brethren (the icy kind) and the perilous Yeti. The glaciers are populated after all ....

The journey through the slippery caverns seems fairly straightforward, other than battling the enemies you run across. Negotiating your way through splintered airships, you eventually stumble upon the legendary City of the Ancients. You suspect that there's more going on behind these metallic walls than you first thought. Why else would someone place an active generator here?

From within the glacial caves, you pick a perfect moment to eavesdrop on several Legionnaires. You find out that Necros' minions are excavating crashed airships and restoring them to working condition. Toward what purpose, you still don't know — but it can't be good.

An army of revenants awaits you in the not-so-vacant excavation site. Fighting your way through them, you discover the body and battle-ready soul of the Revenant Captain. After a harrowing fight, you release his imprisoned spirit and lay claim to the treasured Star of Erathia. Perhaps *now* Celestia will show a little gratitude.

Any fleeting hope you have is quickly dashed, though, when the Old Guard Crusader relays another one of Celestia's hand-picked quests and shuttles you back to Duskwood.

As you leave the ferry, you see the Talisman of Storms (Air Armor) to your left. Ignore the other floating platforms, and jump straight to the island with the talisman.

Just as you enter the ice cave, take a quick right and save — just to be safe.

Now, prepare for an icy slide down the cave.

GLACIERS

Watch for a hidden alcove on the top of the passage. If you time your jump correctly, you can grab a light gem.

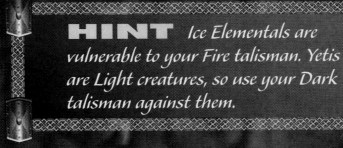

HINT Ice Elementals are vulnerable to your Fire talisman. Yetis are Light creatures, so use your Dark talisman against them.

Exit the ice cave, take care of a few more Ice Elementals, and take a look around.

You'll come to an ice wall, but it's unbreakable.

Instead, enter the crashed airship to your left.

There's a small wooden door to your right.

Break it down and go in.

The ice gives way to a metal chamber and a Glacial Elemental — taller and more powerful than any other Elemental you've seen so far.

TIP Glacial Elementals cast Snap Freeze, which temporarily paralyze you. Get in as many blows as you can in between his spells. You can't consume potions while you're frozen, so boost your health before this fight begins.

11

Take a peek in the ice-covered passage and get rid of the pesky Ice Elemental guarding it.

12

Follow the metal passageway. It looks safe enough, but you'll find two Yeti hanging out in an open metal chamber just ahead.

13

Now, for a little crate-pushing ... shove it up against the entryway (so you can climb back out).

14

Hit the switch in the little room, then hop on the box and make a beeline for the metal chamber.

15

Pass through the newly opened door. It only stays open for a short time — if it's closed, go back and hit the switch again.

Encounters

GLACIAL ELEMENTAL (8)
8 - 2 Water Gem

ICE ELEMENTAL (13)
13 - Water Gem

OLD GUARD CRUSADER (1)
1 - 9g, Spirit Gem, 2 ThrAx

YETI (6)
Most have Light Gem.
1 - 121 g
1 - 125g, Healing p
2 - 132g
1 - 117g
1 - 123 g

YETI LORD (6)
All have Mind Gem.
1 - 131g, Restore p
1 - 171, 2 Restore p
1 - 183g, 2 Restore p
1 - 194g, Restore p
1 - 201g, 2 Restore p
1 - 166g, 2 Restore p

YETI SHAMAN (1)
1 - Holy Wrath s,
2 Light Gem, Light Armor t

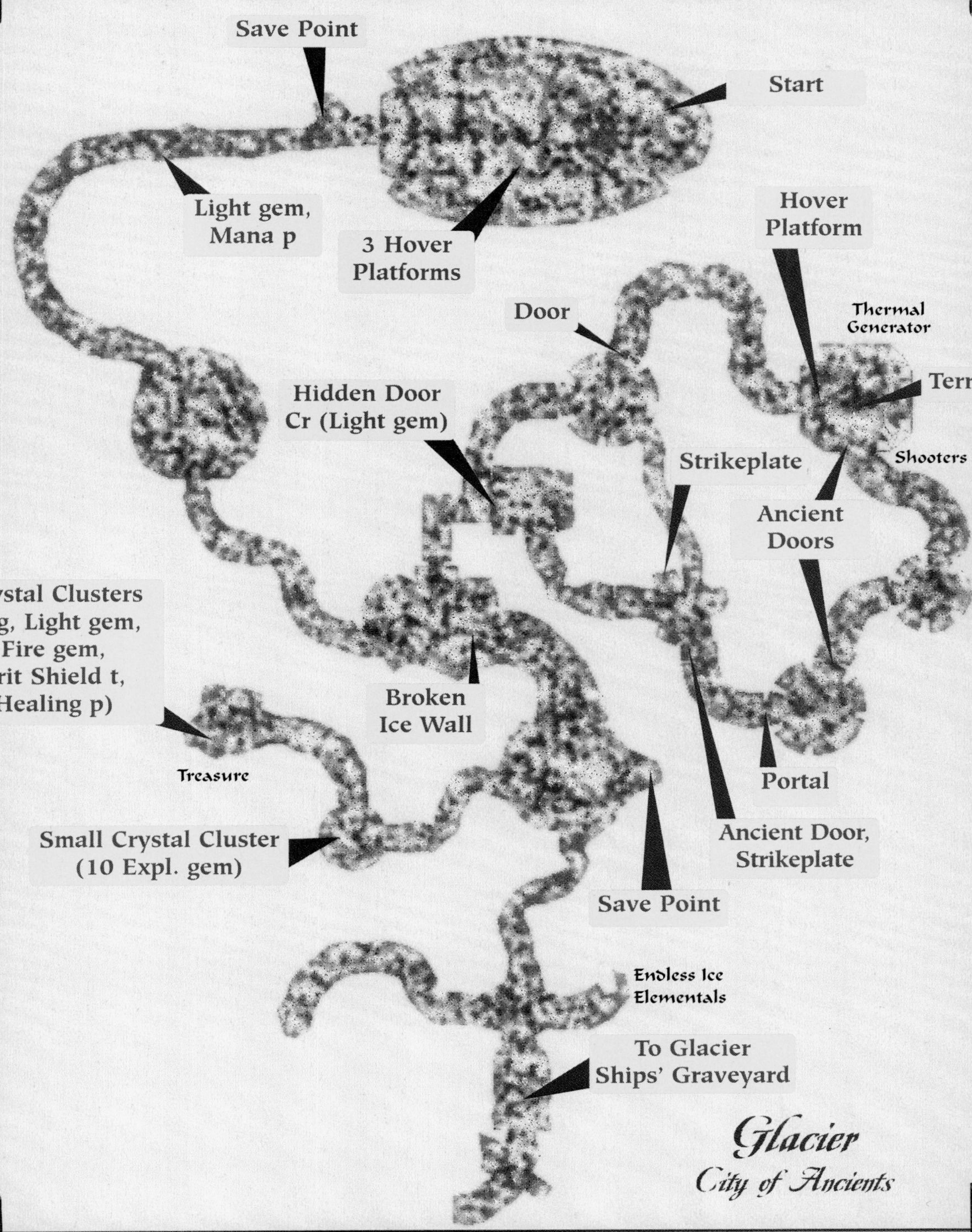

Save Point

Start

Light gem,
Mana p

3 Hover
Platforms

Hover
Platform

Door

Thermal
Generator

Terraformer

Hidden Door
Cr (Light gem)

Strikeplate

Shooters

Ancient
Doors

3 Crystal Clusters
(210g, Light gem,
3 Fire gem,
Spirit Shield t,
2 Healing p)

Broken
Ice Wall

Treasure

Small Crystal Cluster
(10 Expl. gem)

Portal

Ancient Door,
Strikeplate

Save Point

Endless Ice
Elementals

To Glacier
Ships' Graveyard

Glacier
City of Ancients

GLACIERS

16

Defeat the Yeti that greets you and follow the Hall of Geothermal Power. Once you spot the tall machine, watch out for *Lightning* strikes from the middle tower.

Step gently over the edge and drop down to a ledge to take on another Yeti. If you fall to the bottom, hop onto the stone elevator to get back to the ledge.

17

Now, you must fight the Yeti Shaman. Attack from the ledge with a *Fire Storm* spell and suffer *Lightning* attacks, or face him at ground level with your Nightbringer (Dark Weapon) Talisman.

18

The Yeti Shaman eventually coughs up a Talisman of Teruvia (Light Armor) and *Holy Wrath* spell. Your spell collection is now complete!

19

Take the elevator back up, then run around the ledge.

20

Walk out to the center platform. You'll automatically toss four Light gems into a hopper to activate the generator.

21

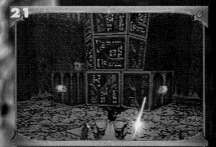

Be bold and jump down to the bottom level ...

22

... and go through the open door. Run through the hallway in short spurts, timing your runs through a field of exploding gems.

TIP *This is a good time to boost your Health up as much as you can. And since your next opponents make a deadly team, focus on killing them one at a time.*

23

The exit from the circular room ahead of you is blocked by an impenetrable green force field.

24 The room contains a Glacial Elemental and a gem in the center of the room that shoots *Lightning* bolts at you. You can't leave until the Elemental is dead.

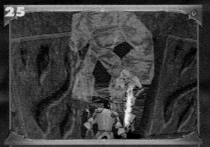

25 Follow the hallway. A dangerous duo awaits in the next chamber — a Glacial Elemental who *Snap Freezes* you, and a Yeti Lord who will then hit you with a *Holy Wrath* spell.

26 Follow the passageway until you reach a locked door. Just to the left, you'll find a switch that opens it.

27 Ah, the look of familiar territory … and another Yeti Lord to defeat. He's not nearly as tough as the last one, though.

Once he's dead, turn left and exit the wrecked airship.

28 Inspect the ice wall closely — the generator has cracked it. A few good whacks with Flamefang, your Fire Talisman weapon, will finish the job.

29 A Yeti, Ice Elemental and Glacial Elemental await you. Get rid of them, and then take the time to find the Save Point in the chamber.

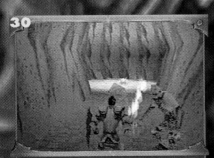

30 This chamber has two passages. The one straight across from the Save Point is optional, but rewarding.

31 When you take down the two Ice Elementals and two Glacial Elementals, take a closer look at the two glowing jewels. Shatter the jewels to reveal gold, gems, potions and the (Astral Rune) Spirit Shield Talisman.

32 Return to the crossroads and head for the exit.

GLACIERS

85

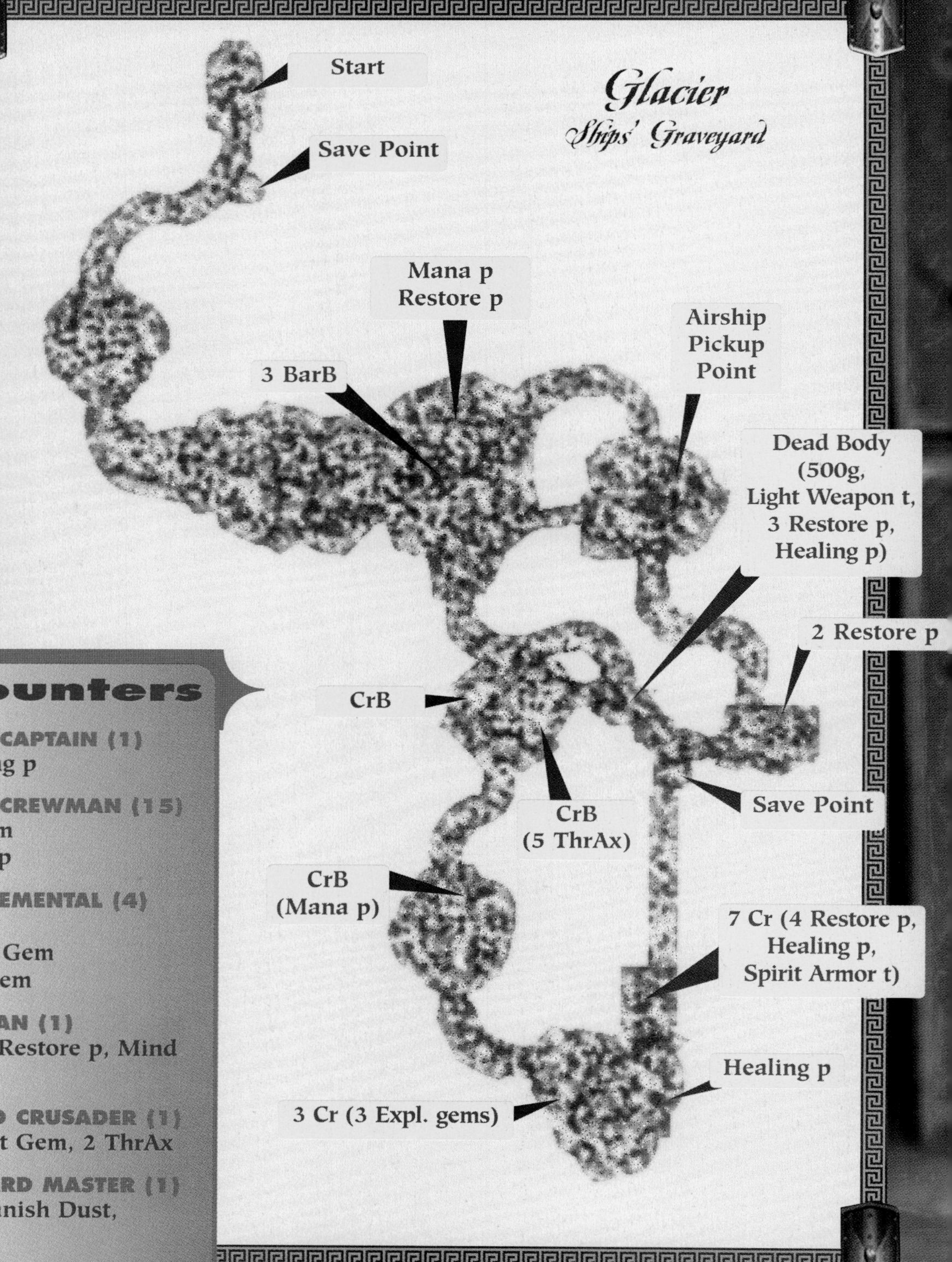

GLACIERS

Glacier
Ships' Graveyard

Start

Save Point

Mana p
Restore p

3 BarB

Airship
Pickup
Point

Dead Body
(500g,
Light Weapon t,
3 Restore p,
Healing p)

2 Restore p

CrB

CrB
(5 ThrAx)

Save Point

CrB
(Mana p)

7 Cr (4 Restore p,
Healing p,
Spirit Armor t)

Healing p

3 Cr (3 Expl. gems)

Encounters

REVENANT CAPTAIN (1)
1 - 5 Healing p

REVENANT CREWMAN (15)
14 - Air Gem
1 - Restore p

GLACIAL ELEMENTAL (4)
1 - Mana p
1 - 2 Water Gem
2 - Water Gem

YETI SHAMAN (1)
1 - 201g, 2 Restore p, Mind Gem

OLD GUARD CRUSADER (1)
1 - 9g, Spirit Gem, 2 ThrAx

BLACK GUARD MASTER (1)
1 - 261g, Vanish Dust, 3 ThrAx

TWICE-BORN (3)
3 - 105g, 2 ThrAx

33

Near the exit, there's an ice slide. Elementals will continually appear and come down the slide after you. This is a good place to hang out if you want more experience, a bad place if you're hurt or in a hurry.

34

To the right there's another optional passage. It contains a couple of monsters and no special treasure.

35

When you're through fighting, take a deep breath and leap off the ledge.

36

The first thing you'll find on the next level is a Save Point off to the left. Once you've saved, head for the first open area.

37

These opponents should look familiar — yet another Glacial Elemental and Yeti Lord. Use the same tactics you did earlier.

TIP When you walk across the bridge, hold down L2 as you walk. Short baby steps are much safer than your usual gait.

38

The log bridge in front of you allows you to cross the ravine, but you've got to melt down the Ice Elemental that's guarding it first.

39

Keep a steady course until you find yet another crashed airship. Way down at the bottom you'll find two most challenging enemies — the Crusader Revenants.

40

Jump down onto the deck to inspect your new friends. Like most undead creatures, they're rather transparent.

Forget about using normal weapons against them. They are resistant to them, and magical spells as well. Get Bonemender, your Body Weapon Talisman, ready.

GLACIERS

87

GLACIERS

HINT

Revenants are particularly strong. If you keep getting knocked backward, try a jumping attack. They can't knock you back after this attack.

Having claimed victory, you can collect a pair of potions on top of the hull. Use a Dasher Nut paired with a long jump to reach them.

Back on deck, turn to the explosive barrels (marked with Xs). If you hit them just right with your *Fire Storm* spell, the trapdoor in front of you drops open.

Jump down into the hold and look around.

Scroll: The Master has chosen me to oversee your work and to ensure you deliver more Airships on time.

There's a scroll resting in plain sight on top of a box — walk up and read it.

HINT

If you accidentally push the box into a corner, keep pushing. It will eventually slide one way or the other.

A second box in the hold is surrounded by barrels. Smash all but the explosive one (marked with an X).

Push the box over near the large stack of boxes in the middle of the hold. Don't put it too close, though — you're going to need a little room in between. Jump onto the stack, and jump again to the stack near the opening.

Hit the gem with a forceful spell or a thrown weapon. It shoots off a *Lightning* bolt, which destroys the boxes blocking the opening. Enter and follow the icy passage.

48 An Ice Elemental is waiting in the first open area you come to. Enjoy this fight, because this is the last Elemental you'll face.

49 Take a second to notice the ice wall to the right. You'll return here later to meet the Old Guard Crusader, but not until you've retrieved the Star of Erathia.

TIP *Use Oakheart (the Earth Weapon Talisman) and Deadly Swarm spell against the Black Guard Master. Deal with him first, then the Twice-Born.*

50 Go forward and eavesdrop on a Black Guard Master and three Twice-Born talking about the ships. They immediately attack. Kill them, then clamber up to the top of the hull to pick up both a healing and restore potion.

51 Hang a right to find your next Save Point.

52 The quarry-like area you find down the passageway contains three Revenants. Unless you're bent on a suicide mission, don't rush out into battle. Take small steps forward until you trigger the first Revenant. Handling them one at a time is definitely the smartest plan.

53 The passage to your left leads to a fallen mast that is shielding you from a couple of Revenants. You can jump up onto the mast and cast spells at them. Or, you can make a mad dash for the next open area. Revenants aren't that hard to dodge, and if you play your cards right, they might not chase you into the next open area.

HINT *If you get into trouble (i.e., all the Revenants are coming after you), run back to the ship and jump up on the hull. They won't come after you, and you can use spells from a distance. Once you've finished off the Revenants, pick up the Air gems they left behind. If you want a few throwing axes, smash the crate in this area.*

GLACIERS

GLACIERS

54

If you choose to fight them and take a moment to look around, the crate in the passageway contains a mana potion.

55
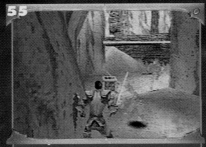
The next area has yet two more Revenants and a well-preserved airship. You can either run right into a melee, or approach slowly to trigger a single Revenant. (If you're trying to outrun the ones in the passage, however, this won't work — they'll follow you and attack.)

HINT Use the terrain in this open area like an obstacle course. You've got crates, an icy incline, and a little running room. Just don't let the Revenants corner you.

56

Push the single crate over near the stacked crates to create steps.

57

Climb up the crates and hop onto the wing. Carefully walk across the log ...

58

... and climb up the slope in front of you to reach the top of the airship.

59

The middle of the airship has a large, deep hole. Go to the right and step off the edge — there's a ledge midway down that you can land on. Try not to fall all the way down — it probably won't kill you, but you'll take some major damage.

60

A lone Revenant is patrolling the hull. Dispose of him and jump down into, yes, yet another hole.

61

Get rid of one more Revenant down here, then read the scroll on top of the crate. It provides you with a clue about how to destroy the Revenant Captain for good. Take mental notes ... you'll need this information later.

62

The other crates contain a couple of nice surprises — a few potions and the Karmic Talisman (Spirit Armor). Once you pick up the loot, drop into the hole.

63

The long ramp in front of you is blocked at the other end with a force field. Your first task at hand, however, is to dispel the two Revenants.

64

Push one of the crates up against the force field. If you wait a few seconds, you'll notice that it's creating an electrical arc.

Repeating this feat with the second crate shorts out the force field altogether, permitting you to continue. Climb up the ramp.

65

Take the doorway to the left. This leads into the room containing the Revenant Captain's dead body and his not-so-dead spirit. He'll start a fight as soon as he sees you. You can fight him as long as you want, but he will simply regenerate and utter "I return!"

66

Once you release the Captain's spirit, he's eternally thankful and drops the Star of Erathia, which also doubles as the Light Weapon Talisman. Make sure you pick up this coveted item — you'll need it later.

TIP *Remember the scroll in the hull? The secret to getting rid of the Captain once and for all is to attack his dead body with either the Fire Storm spell or a weapon armed with the Fire Talisman.*

67

By now you should expect that any open, icy area contains at least a couple of Revenants. You'll be glad to know that these are the the last two you'll ever have to see.

68

Follow the passage upward until you reach the ferry.

69

The Old Guard Crusader is happy to see you and gives you a quick overview of your next mission and a quick tip on what to do with your new Star of Erathia.

The Grub Queen

It appears that the Legion has been using the Grub Cave as an underground supply mechanism to fuel its siege at Stronghold. Celestia wants you pierce the core of the operation and shut it down — whatever that requires. Although more spelunking isn't exactly what you had in mind, you reluctantly agree. At least the climate in Duskwood is an improvement over the glaciers.

The forest is ominously silent when you arrive, except for a lone Ogre or two. Heeding the Old Guard Crusader's advice, you hack and grunt your way into the Grub Cave with your new Star of Erathia.

Poking your way through the dark, tangled cave, you encounter no one other than a few squatty Hive Warriors. The journey seems far too easy, at least until you stumble into the lair of the Grub Queen. You quickly discover that the caves are actually hive tunnels — and that this is the unhappy queen you've disturbed.

Defeating the Grub Queen rouses the Hive Warriors and puts the hive in total chaos. Surely this will disrupt the Legion's precious supply line!

Your mission accomplished, you retrace your steps. The journey back through the hive proves three-fold harder than getting in — the exit is blocked and the warriors are understandedly angry — but you eventually find your way back to Duskwood and the ferry.

Celestia summons you once again to Stronghold ....

The Old Guard Crusader drops you off in Duskwood and instructs you to find the webbed entrance to the cave. Follow the path lined with mushrooms.

An Ogre is guarding the cave entrance, but he's an easy target. Pick up the two throwing axes he drops.

Activate the Light Talisman (the Star of Erathia) and slash through the webbing to expose the cave entrance.

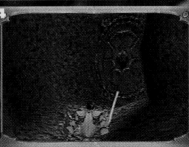

To your right inside the cave is a well-hidden Save Point.

Keep traveling along the cave. You'll soon run across Hive Warriors, little purple creatures that are both fast and hardy.

The first open area has cocoons ... the one on the right holds a Hive Warrior. On the others, use your War Hammer or blunt weapon to get the goodies.

GRUB QUEEN

Travel farther into the cave. The webbing becomes more dense as you approach the Grub Queen's lair, and several more of her loyal Warriors attack you along the way.

HINT *Hive Warriors are Body creatures, which means your Spirit Talisman is a good bet. They don't have any ranged attacks, but they're fairly nimble and love to jump. You'll have to chase them down.*

TIP *If you use a melee weapon and strike the Queen's egg sac, all her resistances drop to 20 for a few seconds.*

Ready your *Lightning* spell, use a mana potion and drop down into the hole to face the Grub Queen.

The Queen is one dangerous lady. She can spit fireballs, attack you with her mandibles, and summon Hive Warriors to defend her. You can't get out of here until she's dead.

The only way to destroy her is to attack her head with *Lightning* strikes or thrown weapons.

Quickly target her head. Get off as many *Lightning* bolts or throwing axes as you can before she starts tossing fireballs your direction and summoning Hive Warriors.

The more of these guys there are, the harder it will be for you to attack her. Keep focused on her — if you kill a Warrior, she calls another one into action.

HINT *You can jump up or cartwheel to the left or right to avoid the Queen's fireballs. She tends to fire off anywhere from five to ten in a row, then takes a break.*

GRUB QUEEN

GRUB QUEEN

12

After you overthrow the Queen, climb the ladder to escape the pit. A few angry Hive Warriors try to stop you, but you can easily make short work of them.

13

Retrace your steps back to the cocoon room. They've webbed shut the passage that leads to the entrance. Instead, take the open path — the one to the right.

14

You soon find an open area that must be the central supply line.

15

Bash almost all of the cocoons. Avoid the cocoon just inside and to the right — it's hiding a Shambler. Break open all of the others to stock up on gold or gems and pick up the Dark Armor Talisman.

16

Go out into the hallway. The Legion was using this tunnel as a supply line, but the Hive Warriors have recently webbed up everything. A few of them drop in to see what you're doing there.

Once you dispose of them, break open the cocoons in the hallway. A few have Shamblers, but your handy Light Talisman can easily take care of them.

17

Go left and follow the hallway. More cocoons, more Warriors … and a couple of crates you can't open.

18

Turn left at the first passageway you run across. It leads back into the cave complex.

19

Save your game and walk out the cave's exit. Eventually, you'll want to follow the trail to the left and return to the ferry.

20

First, if you're missing any talismans, need potions or don't yet own plate armor, take a hike to Corantha or the Dasher village and beef up your inventory.

21

The faithful Guard is waiting to ferry you to the final battle. Climb up the rocks and board the vessel.

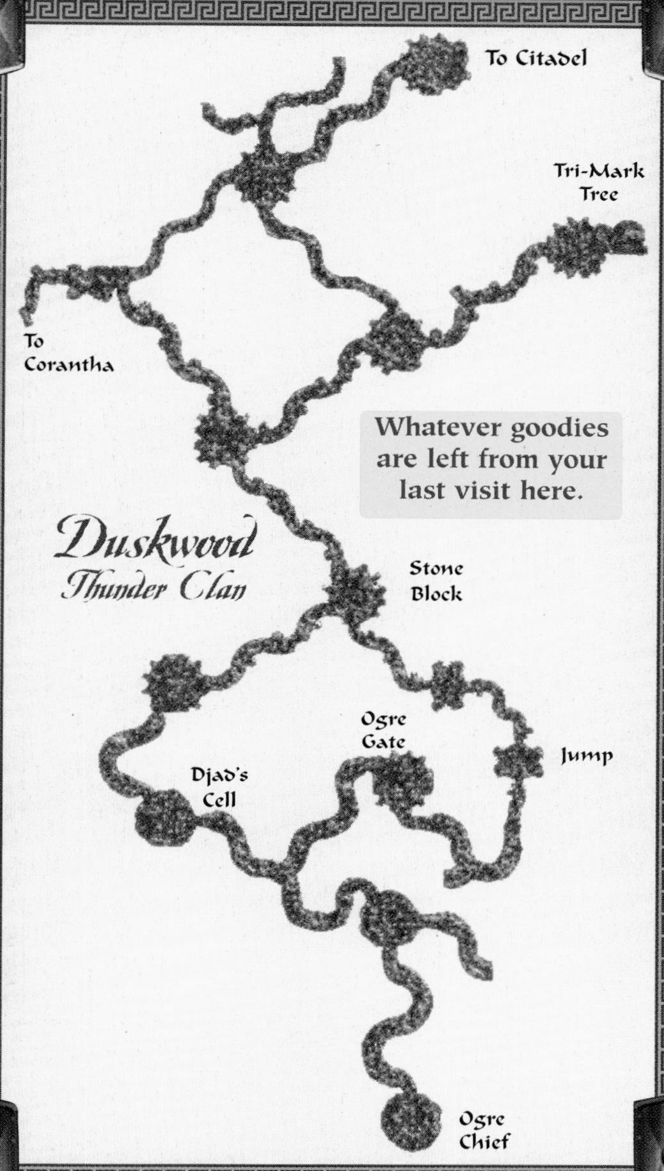

GRUB QUEEN

To Citadel

Tri-Mark
Tree

To
Corantha

Whatever goodies
are left from your
last visit here.

Duskwood
Thunder Clan

Stone
Block

Ogre
Gate

Jump

Djad's
Cell

Ogre
Chief

Encounters

OLD GUARD CRUSADER (1)

1 - 9g, Spirit Gem, 2 ThrAx

Whatever is left from your
last visit here (see p. 67).

(see p. 67)

Duskwood
Grub Hive

Grub Queen's
Lair

o = Cocoons

Encounters

HIVE WARRIOR (36)
36 - 2 Expl. gem

SHAMBLER (3)
3 - 69g

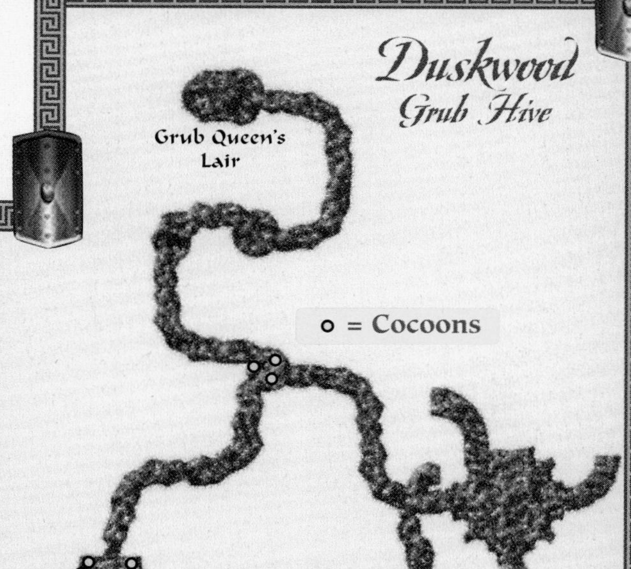

Trench Warfare

Not quite ready to face Celestia, you take a short sojourn at the beach near Citadel to deliver Foss' message to Lt. Shmideck and duck in for a quick visit to the Quartermaster.

An impatient Celestia is waiting at the entrance to Stronghold, but she doesn't seem particularly grateful for your success so far. She now wants information — lots of it, and very quickly. Your new mission is to penetrate enemy lines and spy on the Legion.

Before abandoning the friendly trenches, you check up on your old friend Pollux, the Dwarven Smithy. Quite dejected, he laments Castor's untimely death and blames Captain Ursan and Lady of Archon for a lack of morale among the dwarves. Your kind words ward off desertion, but you silently agree that it all sounds quite suspicious.

You drop quietly behind enemy lines only to face more than a handful of Homunculi. These nasty, hyperactive gremlins are obviously on a mission to distract you. You prefer to focus on the duty at hand. Eventually, your persistence pays off and you confront Necros himself in one of the Legion's antechambers.

The vile leader stays only long enough to boast that his plan is ripening and Citadel has all but been overrun. He claims that you've been properly led astray all this time, then teleports away.

You're left to deal with his Black Guard Heroes and one untimely messenger. You figure that what's good for the messenger can't be too bad for a hero, so you brace yourself and leap into his green teleportal. Within moments, you're transported to an airship docked at Citadel — the same one Necros must have used to hammer his way in.

1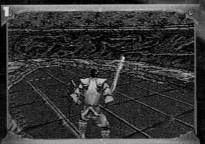

Jump off the ferry and take the elevator down.

2

Exit the compound through the double doors.

3

To your right, there's a guard between two cannon. Deliver the message from Foss. He instructs you to visit the Quartermaster for some needed supplies. Follow the path next to the guard to locate him.

4

The Quartermaster gifts you with 40 exploding gems (save these for much later) and 60 throwing axes.

5

Return to the complex and follow the left path toward Stronghold.

TRENCHES

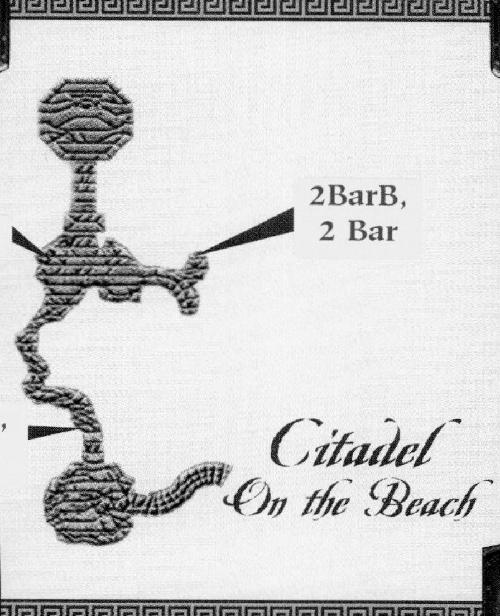

TRENCHES

Cr, 2 BarB

2BarB,
2 Bar

4 Bar, BarB,
1 BarB, Cr

Citadel
On the Beach

Encounters

CRUSADER HIGH GUARD
3 - 9g, Dark Gem

CRUSADER OLD GUARD
10 - 9g, Spirit Gem, 2 ThrAx

Encounters

**BLACK GUARD
HERO (2)**
2 - 201g, Vanishing
    Dust, 2 Expl. gem

DARK LORD (2)
2 - 489g, 2 Healing p,
    2 Expl. gem

DARK MAGE (2)
1 - 149g
1 - 489g,
    Resurrection p,
    Dark Gem

**BLACK GUARD
SENTRY (4)**
2 - 9g, Dark Gem
2 - 149g, 2 ThrAx

HOMUNCULOUS (11)
Most have 261g.
1 - Mana p, Mind
    Gem
1 - Dark Shield t,
    Mind Gem
4 - Mana p, Mind
    Gem
5 - 55g

SHAMBLER (2)
1 - 149g, 2 ThrAx
2 - 261g, Mana p,
    Mind Gem

**STONEHEART
REGULAR (2)**
2 - 9g, 3 ThrAx

OLD GUARD (8)
5 - 9g, Spirit Gem, 2
    ThrAx

BIGGLES
1 - 9g, Spirit Gem, 2
    ThrAx

SARGE
1 - 9g, Spirit Gem, 2
    ThrAx

TRENCHGUARD
1 - 9g, Spirit Gem, 2
    ThrAx

POLLUX
1 - 9g, 3 ThrAx

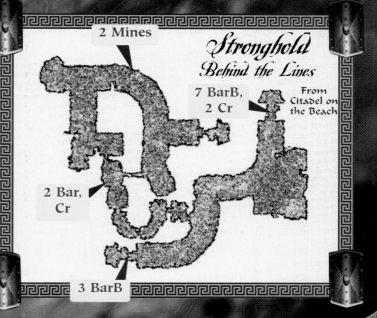

2 Mines

7 BarB,
2 Cr

From
Citadel on
the Beach

2 Bar,
Cr

Stronghold
Behind the Lines

3 BarB

TRENCHES

6 Make a quick pit stop at the Save Point.

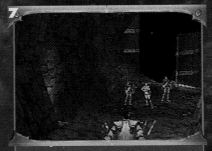

7 Celestia and two guards greet you. She urges you to penetrate behind enemy lines as far as possible.

8 Save again for safety's sake.

9 You're faced with two paths. The right one is optional, but useful — visit it first.

10 Follow the right path until you reach the trench, then jump down. Go left all the way to the tower.

11 Several dwarves, including Pollox, greet you with dim spirits. After muttering something about a dwarven desertion, he gives you Razor's Edge (Mind Weapon) which is probably your only missing talisman.

12 Return to the trench entrance and climb back up.

13 Follow the left path.

14 When you find the Guard with the cannon, he warns you not to enter. Do it anyway — it's time to enter enemy territory.

Dust off, then head down the hallway.

Turn right.

The hallway turns to the right again. Just past the turn you'll find another save point.

HINT Homunculi are agile, resistant to every type of damage and magic, and spend most of their time giggling and dodging your attacks. Homunculi also love to cast Deadly Swarm spells against you. If you do manage to lower their health, they tend to run away and heal themselves with Regeneration. They do have one weakness — on occasion, they'll get stuck trying to run through a wall.

Keep going down the hallway until you see an open doorway on the left side. Pass through it.

Go down the hallway until you encounter a Black Guard Sentry and a Homunculus.

After you finish them off, head for the next room and get rid of another Black Guard Sentry.

Climb up the ladder.

As you go down the hallway, try to pin the three Homunculi down in a corner and whack them to death, using long-range spell attacks when they run away from you.

The open room down the hallway has a Lightning trap that fires from above, along with more Homunculi.

TRENCHES

TRENCHES

24

The other end of the room has a small area containing several crates and a suit of Black Guard Armor.

25

It's not as much of a dead-end as it looks. Pick up the armor, then break the boxes to expose a hidden exit.

26

It drops into an enemy trench. Go left and do your best to avoid the Homunculi.

27

The trench has a fork to the right. Follow it all the way into the outpost.

28

Kill the Homunculi to get the Dark Shield Talisman, Rune of Shadow. Beware the open window, however ....

29

Go back to the fork and turn right. Keep going, then take the fork to the left.

30

You'll find an outpost with a few Black Guard Sentries. There's a locked door behind them that you can't open.

31

Go back to the fork and turn left. A few steps down, you'll find another pair of sentries and an entrance.

32

Inside the entrance, you'll find a save point.

33

Squeeze through the crack in the back wall and walk up to the ladder.

34

You're met by two Black Guard Heroes and another stranger, the Dark Mage. You can't hide. A Level 5 Holy Wrath spell is your best bet.

35

Once you slay your three enemies, pick up their gold and their Vanish Dust. The doorway to the right is now open. Go through it.

36

Within this chamber you find Necros himself. He makes a little speech and teleports away.

37

He rudely leaves you to the mercies of a Dark Mage and Dark Warlord. Holy Wrath, Holy Wrath, Holy Wrath … three or four successive castings should do it.

38

One last Dark Warlord appears, expecting to find Necros. Kill him, then walk through the green gate to exit the Stronghold.

39

It's back to Citadel …

40

… and to five Homunculi waiting for you on the airship's deck. You can either try to run past them out onto the ship's wing, or take care of them here.

41

Aerrin's flown down on the ferry to pick you up and give you the scoop on your next mission. Jump onto it, but be wary of any Homunculi that remain. Their Deadly Swarm spell can cause you to miss your jump.

Free Citadel from Necros

NECROS

Despite an unfriendly greeting from the Homunculi, you spot Aerrin's ferry at Citadel and jump aboard. She bears unsettling news; the Legion of the Fallen has taken over the Light Lance and turned it against the Old Guard. You fear time is running out for the Crusade, but agree to do your best to disable the lance.

Shorting out the Light Lance should be as easy as switching off a pair of control gems and switches. It is ... except for the loyal Black Guard Heroes who've been appointed to guard it with their lives.

Finally, mission accomplished! Now, it's time to corner Celestia and turn these haphazard facts into some sort of truth.

To your dismay, the Royal chambers have been overrun by Black Guard Heroes. Even Celestia's bedroom appears strangely empty, except for the Guardian statues who come alive in her defense.

An accidental visit to Citadel's rooftop deepens the mystery. While you've been galavanting around risking life and limb for the Crusade, someone's been rebuilding the Kreegan device. This interdimensional portal that allowed Ancients and Kreegans to travel here must be kept dismantled and destroyed beyond repair. It must be not be allowed to be used again. The danger is tremendous, since any operator of the Kreegan device can absorb unlimited power. What's worst of all, this repair is happening right under Celestia's nose!

Not surprisingly, Necros makes another appearance on the roof. He douses your hopes even further with crushing news of manipulation and deceit within the very halls of Citadel. Necros reveals his grand plan to harness the power of the Kreegan interdimensional gateway, and heartily scoffs at your attempt to stop him. The future looks bleaker than ever. Have you and the entire Crusade really been no more than simple pawns in a tug-of-war between Celestia and Necros?

Necros' conquest appears to be complete as he summons up a swirling whirlwind in the skies over Citadel. But in true Crusader form, you figure out a way to snatch victory from his grasp at the last desperate moment. Unable to escape his vortex gone awry, Necros is sucked up into its center and disappears.

Barely avoiding Necros' fate, you end up planted face-first on the rooftop with all limbs still attached. Just surviving the last five minutes should make you happy enough. Still ... you have a nagging suspicion that all is not well. There's still no sign of Celestia, and you're left with far more questions than answers. But with Necros gone, Citadel is safe — at least for the time being.

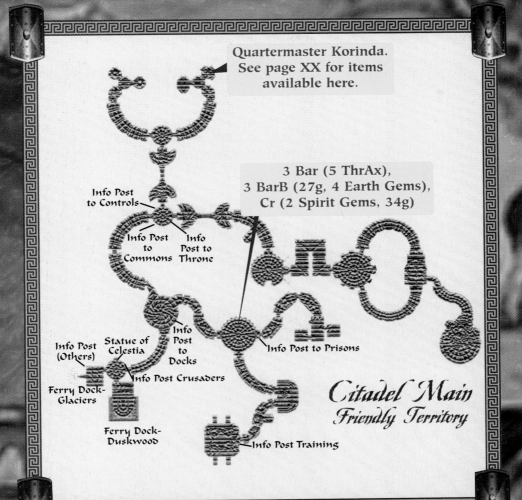

Quartermaster Korinda.
See page XX for items
available here.

3 Bar (5 ThrAx),
3 BarB (27g, 4 Earth Gems),
Cr (2 Spirit Gems, 34g)

Info Post
to Controls

Info Post
to
Commons

Info
Post to
Throne

Info Post to Prisons

Info Post
(Others)

Statue of
Celestia

Info
Post
to
Docks

Info Post Crusaders

Ferry Dock-
Glaciers

Ferry Dock-
Duskwood

Info Post Training

Citadel Main
Friendly Territory

NECROS

Now, step up to the gem
platform and jump up.

Run up the ramp.

Enter the Guard room.

4

Finish off the Homunculi and head down the hallway.

5

The ramp room has three more Homunculi ... the last ones you'll have to deal with.

6

Another Save Point is under the ramp, straight across from the room's entrance.

HINT *If you can lure the Black Guard Heroes down the passage to the left and across the bridge, where two more wait, you can hit all four at once with Holy Wrath — but it's not easy.*

7

The passageway to the right is useless. Instead, head up the ramp.

8

There's a Black Guard Hero at the first archway – kill him and go to the intersection.

9

This intersection has two more Black Guard Heroes, and a passageway to the left.

10

After the fight, put the original entrance behind you, and then take a left.

11

Cross the bridge. The force field that once guarded the Light Lance is now off.

12

After you take care of two more Black Guard Heroes, take a right. Go to the bridge.

NECROS

13

Across the bridge are two Black Guard Masters and a Dark Mage. As usual, use *Holy Wrath* against them.

14

In the adjacent bridge room is a scroll that says the switches both control gems. Both must be turned off to deactivate the Light Lance.

15

Hit the switch to turn it off.

16

Hit the gem — it turns dark.

17

Turn back toward the intersection and go forward to the other "wing."

18

You'll find a repeat situation. Two Dark Lords, not much room, and a gem/switch combination.

19

After you've killed the Lords, deactivate the second gem.

20

Throw the second switch. Finally, the Light Lance is off!

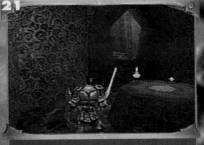

21

Go back to the intersection.

22

Turn right — you're on your way out now.

23

Go back across the bridge …

24

… turn left …

NECROS

25 ... cross another bridge, and pause to deal with a single Black Guard Master.

26 Up the hallway, you'll find the last Save Point of the game. Save. Definitely. Then follow the hall to the end.

27 Two Dark Lords are there, plus a Black Guard Hero at a cannon. Rush across to the far wall — it's out of range.

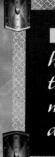

HINT *If you hurry, you can run into the royal hallway to the left without fighting the Dark Lords. Let them chase you into Celestia's throne room (where three more join the chase) and then to her bedroom ... but don't let them catch you!*

28 Take the royal passageway — you can't miss its bright red carpet.

29 Follow the trail of red carpet all the way to Celestia's throne room.

30 You'll find three Black Guard Heroes. This room's big enough that you can run around and cast Holy Wrath as they chase you.

31 When you're done fighting, — or just ready to escape — break into Celestia's bedroom. It's the passageway with the blue security field.

32 Pass through the field (despite the warnings) and head for the bedroom.

33 The statues attack. Run into her room and stay close to the line of statues. *Holy Wrath* is hot if you've got the mana to power it.

NECROS

34 One statue doesn't come to life. Use your weapon to smash it to pieces.

35 Behind the broken statue you'll find a secret passageway. Take it.

36 This large room has an elevator in the middle. Step up (not too close) and wait for it to descend.

37 Ride the elevator up. If you're quick enough you can grab the potions on the small ledges.

38 Well, now — Necros!

After a speech, Necros commands his minions to attack.

39 Necros can't be killed, so don't even try. Also, there is an endless supply of guards. The only way to destroy Necros' invention is to destroy the pillars.

Look upward and target the pillars themselves. They're immune to Fire damage, so you'll have to use exploding gems instead. Hopefully you stocked up on them earlier.

40 A damaged pillar cracks but continues to work. When you break a pillar, the lightning ceases.

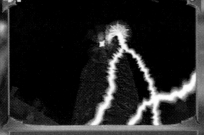

41 To win the game, you must crack all five pillars or break two of them and crack one.

TIP *It's difficult to see what damage you're doing — but perseverance pays off!*

Friend and Foe Vital Statistics

Name	LVL	XP	Health	Str	Damage Bonus (%)		Resistances									
					Melee	Ranged	Normal	Fire	Earth	Air	Water	Body	Spirit	Mind	Light	Dark
CRUSADERS																
Aerrin	—	—	700	36	20	10	100	100	100	100	100	100	100	100	100	100
High Guard Crusader	—	—	650	36	20	10	70	55	55	55	55	56	55	55	55	55
Korinda, Crusader Quartermaster	—	—	340	36	20	10	80	75	75	76	75	75	75	75	75	75
Old Guard Crusader	—	—	700	36	20	10	60	40	40	40	40	41	40	40	40	40
Quartermaster	—	—	700	36	20	10	60	40	40	40	40	41	40	40	40	40
Celestia, the Lady Archon	—	—	720	54	50	10	100	100	100	100	100	100	100	100	100	100
Chamber Guardian	10	10000	500	60	60	10	100	85	85	85	85	85	100	85	85	85
Ursan, Captain. of the Crusade	—	—	1000	60	60	10	100	100	100	100	100	100	100	100	100	100
DASHERS																
Dasher Brute	4	1600	400	60	60	10	55	60	60	60	60	40	100	40	60	60
Dasher Scout	3	900	300	50	90	60	45	40	40	40	40	20	100	20	40	40
Dasher Ranger	5	2500	450	60	110	60	65	65	65	65	65	40	100	40	65	65
Tamris, Dasher Chieftain	—	—	1500	60	110	60	65	55	55	55	100	30	100	30	55	55
DWARVES																
King Aiden Stoneheart, Master of Corantha	8	6400	1500	60	60	10	85	65	65	65	100	100	65	50	50	100
Stoneheart Regular	—	—	400	55	100	60	60	65	100	45	65	65	65	65	65	65
General Martel, Warlord of Corantha	—	—	400	55	100	60	100	100	100	100	100	100	100	100	100	100
Castor and Pollux, Dwarven Smithies	—	—	700	55	100	60	60	65	100	45	65	65	65	65	65	65
Crown Prince Dain Stoneheart	—	—	750	55	100	60	100	100	100	100	100	100	100	100	100	100
Prince Tor Stoneheart	—	—	680	55	100	60	100	100	100	100	100	100	100	100	100	100
Ironpick Mage	4	1600	250	40	20	10	40	55	55	55	55	35	55	80	55	55
Ironpick Rebel	2	400	300	45	30	10	60	50	50	50	50	30	50	80	50	50
Ironpick Zealot	3	900	200	50	60	30	50	45	45	45	45	25	45	90	45	45
ELEMENTALS																
Ice Elemental	5	2500	400	60	60	10	70	40	70	70	100	60	60	60	60	60
Lava Elemental	6	3600	400	60	60	10	60	100	70	50	35	55	55	55	55	55
Stone Elemental	5	2500	400	65	60	10	65	70	100	35	50	50	60	60	60	60
Glacial Elemental	6	3600	700	85	100	10	70	40	70	70	100	60	60	60	60	60
Stone Elemental Lord	10	10000	2500	85	100	10	70	80	100	40	80	65	65	65	65	65

Vital Statistics, cont'd

Name	LVL	XP	Health	Str	Damage Bonus (%) Melee	Ranged	Resistances Normal	Fire	Earth	Air	Water	Body	Spirit	Mind	Light	Dark
GRUB																
Hive Warrior	6	3600	700	60	60	10	75	70	70	70	70	100	70	50	70	70
Queen	10	4000	800	-na-	50	10	70	70	70	70	70	70	70	70	70	70
LEGION OF THE FALLEN																
Shambler	4	1600	150	30	0	0	30	25	25	25	25	25	25	25	10	45
Twice Born Fighter	5	2500	250	45	30	10	55	45	45	45	50	45	45	45	25	80
Twice Born Caster	5	2500	250	45	30	10	55	45	45	45	50	45	45	45	25	80
Homunculus Spellcaster	8	6400	600	50	40	10	75	90	70	70	90	90	50	90	70	70
Homunculus Fighter	8	6400	600	50	40	10	75	90	70	70	90	90	50	90	70	70
Black Guard Sentry	6	3600	400	60	70	20	50	60	15	100	75	60	60	60	60	60
Black Guard Hero	7	4900	600	70	80	20	55	65	35	100	80	65	65	65	65	65
Black Guard Master	8	6400	750	80	100	20	60	70	45	100	85	70	70	70	70	70
Final Dark Mage	12	14400	1000	65	80	30	65	75	75	75	85	75	75	75	60	100
Dark Mage	11	12100	800	65	80	30	65	75	75	75	85	75	75	75	60	100
Necros	20	40000	2000	75	100	30	70	70	70	70	85	70	70	70	60	100
Final Dark Lord	12	14400	1200	90	130	30	80	75	75	75	85	75	75	75	50	95
Dark Lord	11	12100	1000	90	130	30	80	75	75	75	85	75	75	75	50	95
OGRES																
Ogre Shaman	5	2500	550	60	100	50	75	50	60	60	60	90	60	40	60	60
Ogre Clansman	3	900	500	65	100	50	75	50	60	60	60	90	60	40	60	60
Ogre Clan Leader	9	8100	1500	80	140	60	80	50	60	60	60	90	60	45	60	60
REVENANTS																
Revenant Captain	10	10000	1500	42	30	10	100	65	65	65	100	50	100	50	65	50
Revenant Crewman	7	4900	600	70	70	10	100	65	65	65	100	50	100	50	65	50
Yeti Lord	9	8100	2000	100	160	50	75	55	70	70	100	70	70	70	100	45
Yeti Shaman	7	4900	600	80	130	50	70	50	70	70	100	70	70	70	100	40
Yeti	6	3600	550	80	130	50	65	45	65	65	100	65	65	65	100	35

Friend and Foe Items

Name	Attack Pref	Attacks	Shield	Spells	Possible Aids	Usual Possessions
CRUSADE						
Aerrin	Spell	Fist (25-45)	—	Lightning (2) Heroism (4)	Restore Potion (10)	
Celestia, the Lady Archon	Spell	Fist (25-45)(Spirit)	—	Deadly Swarm (3) Fire Storm (3)	Restore Potion (10)	
Chamber Guardian	Melee	Fist (25-45)(Light)	—	Lightning (2) or Deadly Swarm (2)		
High Guard Crusader	Melee	Longsword	Kite	—	Restore Potion (5)	10 Gold Dark Gem
Korinda, Crusader Quartermaster	Spell	Fist (25-45)	—	Deadly Swarm (4)	Healing Potion (20)	10 Gold
Old Guard Crusader	Melee	Longsword Throwing Axe	Tower	—	Healing Potion (5)	10 Gold Spirit Gem Throwing Axe
Ursan, Capt. of the Crusade	Melee	Longsword Throwing Axe (Light)	Crusader	—	Healing Potion (10)	
DWARVES						
Castor and Pollux Dwarven Smithies	Melee	Short Axe Exploding Gem	Crusader	—	Healing Potion (15)	10 Gold 5 Exploding Gems
Crown Prince Dain Stoneheart	Melee	Warhammer (Mind)	Tower	—	Healing Potion (30)	
General Martel, Warlord of Corantha	Melee	Warhammer Throwing Axe	Tower	—	Healing Potion (5)	
King Aiden Stoneheart, Master of Corantha	Spell	Warhammer (Dark)	—	Holy Wrath (2)	—	3 Dark Gems
Prince Tor Stoneheart	Melee	Short Axe	—	Deadly Swarm (1) Regeneration (1)	Restore Potion (30)	
Stoneheart Regular	Melee	Warhammer Throwing Axe	Tower Tower	—	Healing Potion (5) Healing Potion (5)	10 Gold 3 Throwing Axes
Ironpick Mage	Spell	Fist (25-45)	—	Lightning (1) Fire Storm (1) Regeneration (1)	Restore Potion (10)	70 Gold Body Gem Restore Potion
Ironpick Rebel	Melee	Short Axe or Mace Throwing Axe	Spiked	—	Healing Potion (5)	20 Gold 2 Throwing Axes Mana Potion
Ironpick Zealot	Ranged	Fist (25-45) Exploding Gem	—	—		40 Gold Exploding Gem
DASHER						
Dasher Brute Healing Potion	Melee	Club	Spiked	—	Vanishing Dust (5)	70 Gold, Earth Gem
Dasher Ranger	Spell	Longsword (Body)	—	Deadly Swarm (1) Heroism (1)	Vanishing Dust (10)	100 Gold Spirit Gem Mana Potion
Dasher Scout	Melee	Short Axe Throwing Axe	—	—	Vanishing Dust (5)	40 Gold 2 Throwing Axes Vanishing Dust
Tamris, Dasher Chieftain	Spell	Longsword (Earth)	—	—	Restore Potion (10)	
ELEMENTAL						
Glacial Elemental	Spell	Fist (35-80) (Water)	—	Snap Freeze (2)		2 Water Gems
Ice Elemental	Melee	Fist (30-60)	—	—		Water Gem
Lava Elemental	Spell	Fist (30-60) (Fire)	—	Fire Storm (2)		Fire Gem, Mana Potion
Stone Elemental	Melee	Fist (30-60)	—	—		Earth Gem Restore Potion

Items, cont'd

Name	Attack Pref	Attacks	Shield	Spells	Possible Aids	Usual Possessions
GRUBS						
Hive Warrior	Melee	Fist (30-60)	—	—	Dasher Nut (5)	2 Exploding Gems
Queen	—	—	—	Fire Storm (4)	—	—
LEGION						
Black Guard Master	Melee	Battle Axe Exploding Gem (Spirit)	Tower	Lightning (2) Heroism (2)	Vanish Dust (10)	260 Gold Vanish Dust Throwing Axe
Black Guard Sentry	Melee	Longsword Throwing Axe	Tower	—	Vanish Dust (5)	150 Gold Throwing Axe
Black Guard Hero	Melee	Longsword (Dark) Throwing Axe	Tower	Lightning (1) Regeneration (2)	Vanish Dust (10)	200 Gold Vanish Dust Exploding Gem
Dark Lord	Melee	Warhammer Freezeball (Dark)	Tower	Lightning (2) Mana Shield (2)	Healing Potion (5)	490 Gold 2 Healing Potions Exploding Gem
Dark Mage	Spell	Fist (30-60)	—	Fire Storm (2) Lightning (2) Regeneration (2)	Restore Potion (5)	490 Gold Restore Potion Dark Gem
Final Dark Lord	Melee	Battle Axe Freezeball (Body)	Tower	Snap Freeze (3) Mana Shield (3)		3 Exploding Gems
Final Dark Mage	Spell	Longsword	—	Fire Storm(3) Lightning (3)		
Homunculus Fighter	Melee	Fist (Earth)	—	—	Dasher Nut (5)	260 Gold Mana Potion Mind Gem
Homunculus Spellcaster	Spell	Fist (30-60)	—	Deadly Swarm (2) Fire Storm (2) Regeneration (3)	Dasher Nut (5)	260 Gold Mana Potion Mind Gem
Necros	Spell	Fist (Air)	—	Lightning (4) Deadly Swarm (3) Heroism (4)		
Shambler	Melee	Mace	—	—		70 Gold
Twice Born Caster	Spell	Fist (30-60)	—	Fire Storm (1)		100 Gold Dark Gem
Twice Born Fighter	Melee	Mace Throwing Axe	Spiked	—		100 Gold 2 Throwing Axes
OGRES						
Ogre Clan Leader	Melee	Battle Axe (Earth)	—	Deadly Swarm (2) Regeneration (3)	Healing Potion (10)	1000 Gold Healing Potions Earth Gem
Ogre Clansman	Melee	Club	—	—		40 Gold 2 Throwing Axes
Ogre Shaman	Spell	Club (Air)	—	Fire Storm (2) Regeneration (1)		100 Gold 2 Restore Potions
REVENANTS						
Revenant Captain	Spell	Longsword (Light)	Crusader	Holy Wrath (2)		5 Spirit Gems
Revenant Crewman	Melee	Longsword	Crusader	—		Air Gem
YETI						
Yeti	Melee	Fist (30-60) Freezeball	Spiked	—		150 Gold Light Gem
Yeti Lord	Melee	Fist (30-60) (Light)	—	Holy Wrath (3) Regeneration (2)		2000 Gold 5 Mana Potions Spirit Gem
Yeti Shaman	Spell	Fist (30-60) (Water)	—	Holy Wrath (2)	Restore Potion (5)	200 Gold 2 Restore Potions Mind Gem

Spell Statistics

Spell Name	Mana Cost at Rank					Damage	Duration (secs.)	Radius (feet)	Strength (knockback)	Where first found
	1	2	3	4	5					
Deadly Swarm	40	50	60	70	80	40-70/foe	6 —> 18	15 —> 35	40 —> 60	Duskwood (Djad)
Fire Storm	20	35	50	65	80	60-100/ball	less than a second	30	100	Escape from Stronghold
Holy Wrath	50	70	90	110	130	100-150/foe	0.5 —> 1.5	15 —> 35	100	Glaciers (City of Anc.)
Lightning	25	50	75	100	125	80-120/arc	less than a second	0	50	Corantha (Rebellion)
Snap Freeze	30	40	50	60	70	–	8 —> 16	20 —> 40	–	Corantha (First Visit)
Heroism	30	55	80	105	130	–	60	0	–	Escape from Stronghold
Mana Shield	20	55	90	125	160	–	40 —> 60	0	–	Duskwood (Djad)
Regeneration	40	60	80	100	120	–	30 —> 50	0	–	Dasher Village

APPENDIX